UP THE WINDS *and*
OVER THE TETONS

MAP 1. Portion of Hayden's Geological Map of the Raynolds Expedition. *Hayden Geological Report*, 1869. A portion of this map appears in its original colors on the dust jacket.

UP THE WINDS *and* OVER THE TETONS

JOURNAL ENTRIES AND IMAGES FROM THE 1860 RAYNOLDS EXPEDITION

Edited by

Marlene Deahl Merrill and
Daniel D. Merrill

UNIVERSITY OF NEW MEXICO PRESS

Albuquerque

© 2012 by the University of New Mexico Press
All rights reserved. Published 2012
Printed in the United States of America

17 16 15 14 13 12   1 2 3 4 5 6

Library of Congress Cataloging-in-Publication Data

Raynolds, W. F. (William Franklin), 1820–1894.
Up the winds and over the Tetons: journal entries and images from
the 1860 Raynolds Expedition/William F. Raynolds; edited and
annotated by Marlene Deahl Merrill and Daniel D. Merrill.
        p. cm.
Journals upon which Raynolds later based his Report on the
exploration of the Yellowstone River published in 1868.
Includes bibliographical references and index.
ISBN 978-0-8263-5097-8 (cloth : alk. paper)
ISBN 978-0-8263-5099-2 (electronic)
  1. Raynolds, W. F. (William Franklin), 1820–1894—Diaries.
  2. Yellowstone River Valley—Discovery and exploration—Sources.
  3. Yellowstone River Valley—Description and travel—Sources.
  I. Merrill, Marlene.
 II. Merrill, Daniel D. (Daniel Davy)
III. Raynolds, W.F. (William Franklin), 1820–1894. Report on the
      exploration of the Yellowstone River.
IV. Title.
F737.Y4R39 2012
978.6'3—dc23

                    2011045227

DEDICATED TO J. DAVID LOVE (1913–2002),

LEGENDARY ROCKY MOUNTAIN FIELD GEOLOGIST,

COMMITTED ENVIRONMENTALIST, AND A TRULY FINE MAN.

CONTENTS

ILLUSTRATIONS

Map

FOREWORD

This book reproduces what we believe is the most dramatic portion of Captain William F. Raynolds' handwritten daily journal describing what he and his army exploring party did and saw in portions of present-day Wyoming, Idaho, and Montana from May through early July 1860. It deals with the Raynolds Expedition's travels from its winter quarters near what is today Glenrock, Wyoming, then follows the party's movements northwest up the Wind River Range ("the Winds"), through Jackson Hole, over Teton Pass, and on to the Three Forks of the Missouri in southwestern Montana. Much of this area, with its striking variations in topography and climate, had not previously been explored in a systematic way, if explored at all. Deposited at the Beinecke Rare Book and Manuscript Library at Yale University, Raynolds' narrative is a literate and detailed account of an important but often overlooked expedition, the last major government western expedition before the Civil War.

Although Raynolds did prepare an official government report (*Report on the Exploration of the Yellowstone River*, hereafter referred to as the *Report*), he was not able to complete and publish it until 1868, eight years later. Service in the Civil War, illness, and other duties had kept him from publishing it earlier.

While Raynolds based his *Report* largely on his handwritten journal, there are significant differences between the two. As might be expected, the daily journal entries often possess greater candor and immediacy than do the entries in the *Report*. This is so even though Raynolds sometimes wrote his journal entries for several days at one time.

In addition, Raynolds often altered, removed, or added to his original journal entries. For instance, he omitted from his *Report* all of the daily entries covering his seven-month stay in winter quarters and wrote about this period only in general terms. He also deleted sections from his journal that described the religious services he conducted each Sunday.

There are some serious differences that seem like sizable discrepancies. These are important because most secondary accounts of the

Raynolds Expedition are based on the published *Report* and tend to focus on several "stories" that do not appear in Raynolds' handwritten journal at all. For instance, Raynolds makes no mention in his journal of seeing "a bold conical peak" on May 31, 1860, and naming it "Union Peak" (*Report*, p. 88). It seems unlikely that Raynolds would not have written about seeing and naming this peak in that day's entry, had he done so. A more likely scenario is that he learned about the importance of that peak sometime after the expedition concluded and later embroidered the entry for the published version. This would not be the first time that a personal journal was revised, or even transformed, by a writer while preparing it for publication.

The differences between Raynolds' handwritten journal and his later *Report* are important reasons for publishing this book. As editors, we believe that readers will want to know about these differences.

It should be noted that Raynolds was greatly disappointed with his published *Report*, referring to it as "the abortion Congress published." He had believed it would include a number of images by the two artists on his party—images of the unique landscapes, campsites, and Native Americans seen along the way. He also believed it would include reports from eastern scientists who had examined the expedition's scientific collections (botanical, fossil, geological, animal, and bird) that were sent to them during and immediately after the expedition. But neither the images nor the scientific reports were included in the final *Report*. We have, however, included what we believe are the most striking and important existing images.

Our hope is that, by making Raynolds' original narrative the focus of this book, supplementing it when necessary with segments from his published *Report*, and including the rarely seen images made by the expedition's two artists, we are making available a fuller, more accurate, interesting, and ultimately a more historical account of this important expedition.

ACKNOWLEDGMENTS

The wide-ranging subject matter of this book has led us to seek information, advice, and support from a variety of people: historians, mountain climbers, naturalists, archivists, and art historians. Retracing the Raynolds party's route through Wyoming, Idaho, and Montana was our biggest challenge. Place names had changed through time, and campsites and other locations were often in remote backcountry that is not readily accessible today. We are especially grateful to Tom Turiano, a Teton mountain guide, climber, photographer, historian, and author of *Select Peaks of Greater Yellowstone: A Mountaineering History and Guide*. Tom knows this backcountry well, and he was willing not only to assist us with identifications but also to read and comment on large portions of our manuscript.

We also wish to thank Bill Resor, Jackson Hole rancher and historian (especially of the Raynolds Expedition), who led a three-day workshop on nineteenth-century maps that culminated in a field trip to the area of Union Peak and Union Pass. This renewed our interest in the Raynolds Expedition and helped us to see this important expedition site. Bill also alerted us to the three Schönborn images published in Ferdinand Hayden's *Twelfth Annual Report*.

Ultimately, of course, the identification of specific sites, whether of campsites or expedition routes, rested with us. Besides consulting Tom Turiano and Bill Resor, we also turned to a number of articles and books to help us identify specific locations. Any errors of identification are our responsibility.

We are most grateful to Paul Schullery, scholar-in-residence at Montana State University's Renee Library in Bozeman, Montana, and Lee Whittlesey, Yellowstone Park historian, who not only supported our work from the beginning but also alerted us to the Hutton drawings that are part of the Huntington Library collection in San Marino, California.

Both Peter Blodgett, curator of western American history at the Huntington Library, and George Miles, curator of the Yale Western Americana Collection at the Beinecke Library, assisted and supported us in many ways.

Peter Hassrick, director emeritus of the Denver Art Museum's Petrie Institute of Western American Art, shares our interest in Anton Schönborn and provided us with information about locations where we might find recently available images by Schönborn. Rebecca Lawton, curator of paintings and sculpture at the Amon Carter Museum in Fort Worth, ably assisted us when we examined the museum's collection of Schönborn's watercolors of western forts.

The historian Elizabeth Watry, coauthor of *Images of America: Yellowstone National Park*, provided us with welcome suggestions for textual improvements, sources for images, and current scholarship.

The archival staff at the U.S. Military Academy helped us to access a number of digital files that recorded biographical information about William Raynolds and other West Point graduates mentioned in this book. Our special thanks go to Susan Lintelmann, manuscript curator; Alicia Mauldin-Ware, archives curator; and Valerie Dutdut, Special Collections and Archives Division technician.

Mindy Barnette, Rebecca Stephens, and Shannon Sullivan at the Jackson Hole Historical Society made our research there both easy and pleasant. Elizabeth Menacken, at the National Museum of Wildlife Art in Jackson Hole, provided us with comfortable chairs and an ample table so we could closely examine several published maps.

Our thanks also go to Janet Burkitt, a historical research consultant who investigated and photocopied for us a number of letters written by Ferdinand Hayden to Spencer Baird at the Smithsonian Institution. Her efforts revealed a formerly unknown sketch by Anton Schönborn that illustrates the Raynolds party's winter camp.

Ed Vermue, special collections curator at the Oberlin College Library, provided us with a number of books and maps in his department. He also helped implement the photographing of both maps and chromolithographs by the photographer John Seyfried.

We are grateful for the facilitation of image orders by Karen Nagel at the Beinecke Library, Alan Lutzi at the Huntington Library, Tad Bennicoff at the Smithsonian Institution, and Lisa Keys of the Kansas State Historical Society.

W. Clark Whitehorn, editor-in-chief, and Elizabeth Hadas, director emerita, of the University of New Mexico Press guided our work along the way, making it both enjoyable and more satisfying. We thank Diana Rico for her meticulous copyediting and warm support.

Our friend Lynette Palmer helped us in innumerable ways.

Several unexpected challenges prolonged the completion of this book. Our thanks go to three good friends: the historians Sherry Smith and Bob Righter, and the writer and naturalist Bert Raynes. Their enthusiasm for this work recharged our energies and commitments and helped to keep us going. As always, our thanks also go to our children, Karen and Steve, and their families.

EDITING METHODS

William Raynolds' handwritten field journal can be difficult to read because he often wrote his daily entries when tired and at the end of an arduous day of travel. He saved time by writing abbreviations and incomplete sentences, substituting dashes for periods and commas, or ignoring punctuation altogether. He wrote with few pretensions to creating a literary document. Our editing goal has been to substantially decrease the appearance of page litter and increase the journal's readability. We have therefore spelled out abbreviated words, except for those still in common usage, and then standardized those we have retained. We have completed Raynolds' sentences when his wording is jarring or unclear, incorporated his interlineations into those sentences he clearly wanted them to be a part of, and replaced Raynolds' many dashes with proper punctuation.

Our original transcription was made from a microfilm hardcopy of Raynolds' four journals that are deposited at the Beinecke Rare Book and Manuscript Library at Yale University. We have examined his actual journals at the Beinecke several times to help us identify words that were difficult to make out in the microfilm hardcopy. We refer to these journals as "a journal," since Raynolds' narrative is actually one journal spread out over four volumes. The few words we are still uncertain about appear in roman type in square brackets, and occasionally with a question mark if we are especially unsure. The very few remaining unidentifiable words are signaled with [*illegible word*].

Our editorial insertions appear italicized and within square brackets. These include, for instance, the corrected spelling of names. (Example: "Schonborn [*Schönborn*] went to the bluffs.") Once a name is corrected, it will continue to appear in its corrected form.

Raynolds' spelling is often inconsistent and sometimes unusual—for example, "musquitoes." We have retained his own spelling in his narrative without identifying it with *sic*.

As was the custom of the day, present-day double word place names, such as "Yellowstone," often appeared split with the second word not capitalized, as in "Yellow stone." Names of rivers and mountains almost always appeared without full capitalization, such as "Snake river" instead of "Snake River." Raynolds often did not use *the* when referring to places; for example, he wrote, "We traveled to Wind river." We often inserted *the* in these cases to create smoother reading.

Because Raynolds' journal and his much later published *Report* (which was based on his journal entries) are occasionally dissimilar, we have inserted into his journal narrative portions of his *Report* that either add important new information or differ substantially from his journal accounts. Those *Report* insertions will appear in braces, such as, "It is by far the largest spring of which I have any knowledge, and once seen would not be easily forgotten {and is famous all through this region}." The insertion of such words or passages sometimes required the addition or deletion of insignificant words such as *and*, *the*, and *as* in order to create more readable passages. We have also inserted longer passages from the *Report*, including questionable ones, into the journal narrative. Braces are used for these as well. The important entry from the *Report* for May 31, 1860, is included in full as appendix 1, because it includes so much material not found in Raynolds' handwritten journal.

Place names used in the notes to Raynolds' narrative, or place names that are used in the texts of the introduction and epilogue, will reflect today's usage.

🙥 FIGURE 1. Captain William Franklin Raynolds, circa 1860. Courtesy
of the Library of Congress.

INTRODUCTION

There is a place high astride the Continental Divide in the Rocky Mountains of western America where within a few miles of one another the first trickles of the Snake, the Yellowstone, and the Green Rivers are born. From here everything goes down: to the Columbia, to the Missouri, to the Colorado, and on to the sea. During the exploration of the west, this place, where present-day Wyoming, Idaho and Montana converge, was the last major place to be fitted into the giant puzzle of American geography.

—Rick Reese[1]

In the winter of 1858–1859, William F. Raynolds, a captain in the Corps of Topographical Engineers of the U.S. Army, was stationed in Florida.[2] On April 6, he received a telegram ordering him back to Washington, DC, so that he could prepare to lead a major army expedition in the Intermountain West. In less than two months, he and his party were heading out from St. Louis, intending to spend more than sixteen months in the West, from June 1859 until October 1860.

Funded with a government appropriation of $60,000, the expedition was ordered to explore the region of country "through which flow the principal tributaries of the Yellowstone river, and of the mountains in which they, and the Gallatin and Madison forks of the Missouri, have their source."[3] In doing so, the party would make major contributions to the knowledge of Indian populations and of the geography, geology, and natural history of vast areas of the American West.

This book reproduces what we believe is the most important portion of the four handwritten field journals that Raynolds kept on a daily basis during the expedition. It includes the party's crossing of utterly dry and barren sagebrush plains as well as deep snow-covered mountains and fierce, raging rivers. It exhibits the fortitude of both Raynolds and his party. At the same time, though, it reveals how such physical challenges led to dissension within the group. In short, this portion of Raynolds' journal documents not only a little known piece of western history but also an adventure story full of human interest.

Captain William F. Raynolds and His Orders

Raynolds was thirty-nine at the time of the expedition and a talented and seasoned topographical engineer. When he graduated from West Point in 1843, he ranked fifth in a class of thirty-nine. (His classmate Ulysses S. Grant ranked twenty-first.) He was also ranked first among his classmates for conduct during his final year at West Point. After graduation, he quickly joined the Corps of Topographical Engineers.[4] In this capacity, he had a wide variety of postings: on improvements to the Ohio River, on the Northeastern Boundary Survey, in Mexico during the Mexican-American War, and on surveys to help supply Washington, DC, with water. From 1851 to 1856, he was on the survey of the Northern Lakes, and from 1856 to 1859 he was headquartered in Philadelphia while overseeing the building of lighthouses on the East Coast. He was promoted to captain in 1857.

As varied as these experiences were, they did little to prepare Raynolds for the challenges that he and his intermountain expedition party were to face. He had participated in several extended surveys but had no experience in leading a large expedition into uncharted territory. Although Raynolds had served in Mexico and the Southwest during the Mexican-American War, he had not set foot in that part of the West where he and his party were being ordered to go. Raynolds was more than uneasy about his new responsibilities; as he wrote in his later published *Report*, "My entire want of previous preparation for this duty is offered as an explanation of the many deficiencies that I am conscious exist in the performance of the duties assigned to me."[5]

Raynolds, however, had had one experience that provided some preparation for his new duties. During the Mexican-American War, he was the chief of topographical engineers in Orizaba, southeast of Mexico City. On May 9, 1848, he and six other men made the first recorded ascent of Pico de Orizaba. At over 18,400 feet, this striking volcanic peak is the third highest mountain in North America. (The two tallest peaks, Denali in Alaska and Mount Logan in Canada's Yukon Territory, were not climbed until the twentieth century.) Its peak looms some 16,000 feet above the surrounding valley, more than twice the height of the Grand Teton above Jackson Hole. Raynolds' participation in this demanding climb suggests that he had the personal strength and adventurous spirit that would be needed for his new assignment.[6]

Eleven years later, Raynolds and his men were part of an early governmental effort to explore what was still considered relatively unknown country. Lewis and Clark had explored important areas of the American West in the early 1800s, and accounts by trappers and mountain men had provided additional information. A few rudimentary maps made by adventurous mountain men opened up some of these areas to a diverse group of hunters, trappers, fur traders, and explorers from the late 1820s to the late 1830s. Accurate and detailed descriptions of these regions, however, were few and far between. In fact, after 1840 there was little or no travel to many of these areas by whites, partly because the trapping of beaver virtually ceased once the popularity of beaver hats waned. In addition, more fertile and less mountainous areas attracted greater exploration and eventual settlement because they were far more congenial to farming, ranching, and mining. Few, if any, whites visited Jackson Hole from 1842 to 1859.[7]

Early Western Surveys

Despite the importance of some early written descriptions of these areas, the U.S. government needed more accurate and detailed information about this part of the Intermountain West. In Raynolds' words, "All preliminary information in regard to the interior of this vast region was thus exceedingly vague and unsatisfactory."[8]

An expanding country obviously needed systematic studies. The Corps of Topographical Engineers, which had begun in 1813 and was officially established by Congress in 1838, conducted most of these explorations. The corps was especially active after the full incorporation of Oregon with the treaty of 1846 and the U.S. annexation of much of the Southwest after the Mexican-American War in 1848. This included the four transcontinental railroad surveys of 1853–55, which moved along four different paths from the 32nd parallel in the south to the 47th–49th in the north.

While much of the West had been explored and roughly mapped by 1859, that portion which the Raynolds Expedition was to cover was relatively unexplored. Accounts by trappers and mountain men had provided some information about these areas, but even by 1859 there remained a large swath of terra incognita along the Continental Divide that had yet to be adequately investigated, described, and mapped.

Several expeditions, though, had touched on the area that Raynolds was to explore. A well-known one was that led by Lieutenant John C. Frémont in 1842, with Kit Carson as its guide. The task of this party was to provide information about the route that people were beginning to take to Oregon: specifically, that portion of the route from St. Louis to the Missouri River, and then on to the Platte, North Platte, and Sweetwater rivers, ending up at the South Pass. When he reached the South Pass, however, Frémont decided to explore the western side of the Wind River Range. After making camp at today's Boulder Lake, Frémont and some members of the party climbed what they thought was the highest peak in North America—what is now called Fremont Peak. From its summit, they could see the Tetons to the northwest and the valley of the Wind River on the eastern side of the range. Eighteen years later, the Raynolds Expedition would traverse the Wind River up to its head.[9]

The Raynolds Expedition was the outcome of several explorations led by Lieutenant Gouverneur K. Warren, an 1850 graduate of West Point. In 1855, 1856, and 1857, Warren led successful explorations in Nebraska, South Dakota, and eastern Wyoming. He produced the first accurate map of the area west of the Mississippi River in 1858.[10]

Jim Bridger, the legendary mountain man, accompanied Warren on his expedition in 1856.[11] Bridger so whetted Warren's appetite to explore the upper Yellowstone that Warren presented a detailed proposal for such an exploration to Captain Andrew Atkinson Humphreys of the Corps of Topographical Engineers in November 1858. With his proposal Warren enclosed a small map that showed the southern branches of the Yellowstone River. These, he said, represented only an

> approximation to correctness by using information furnished by the expeditions of Captains Lewis and Clark, and Captain Bonneville, and also from sketches, etc., obtained by me from traders and trappers. This section of the country, however, has much practical importance in relation to routes through it by which to reach Utah from the navigable parts of the Missouri and Yellowstone, and deserves a thorough exploration. . . . [I] have the assurance of the services of Mr. Bridger if the exploration should be ordered.[12]

Warren also justified the need for another expedition on the ground that he expected a "war with the Dakota before many years." He regarded the greatest fruit of his explorations to be the "knowledge of the proper routes by which to invade their country and conquer them." Nonetheless, he added, "I sympathize with them in this their desperation, and almost feel guilty of [a] crime in being a pioneer to the white man who will ere long drive the red man from his last nich [sic] of hunting ground."[13]

However, Warren never led his sought-after expedition, for he was reassigned to West Point to teach mathematics.[14] Instead, in an order dated April 13, 1859, the thirty-nine-year-old Raynolds was ordered by Humphreys (now chief of the topographical engineers) to organize an expedition that would extend Warren's expeditions much further to the West and North.[15]

Raynolds' orders were to explore an area of about 250,000 square miles. More than a little daunted by his upcoming mission, he calculated that he and his party would be exploring a region that was nearly one-fourth larger than all of France and more than double the size of Great Britain.

He also realized that they would be spending over a year and a half in the field, including many months in winter quarters. According to his orders, the objects of the exploration were

> to ascertain, as far as practicable, everything relating to the num-
> bers, habits, and disposition of the Indians inhabiting the country,
> its agricultural and mineralogical resources, its climate and the
> influences that govern it, the navigability of its streams, its topo-
> graphical features, and the facilities or obstacles which the latter
> present to the construction of rail or common roads, either to meet
> the wants of military operations or those of emigration through,
> or settlement in, the country.[16]

All of this turned out to be a considerable challenge for Raynolds and his party.

One of the most important regions that Raynolds was directed to explore was the valley of the upper Yellowstone. Unfortunately, his party, with its heavily packed horses and mules, was unable to reach this area because of an immense amount of snow remaining in early June 1860 around present-day Togwotee Pass—the party's access point into the upper Yellowstone northeast of Jackson Hole. Frustrated, Raynolds and his men were forced to change course, and, with Jim Bridger's guidance, they went through Jackson Hole and never penetrated the area that is now Yellowstone National Park. Had they done so, they would have been acclaimed as the earliest organized party to explore what was to become the world's first national park. Nevertheless, the party's achievements were substantial and deserve greater recognition than they have heretofore received.

The Expedition Party

Early on, Raynolds chose Jim Bridger to be his party's guide, just as Warren had suggested. He understood that Bridger knew, firsthand, many parts of the immense area that his party would explore, even

FIGURE 2. Jim Bridger. Kansas State Historical Society.

though it had been nearly twenty years since he had last been in many parts of it. Raynolds' dependence on Bridger is reflected in the fact that there are over seventy references to him in Raynolds' published *Report* of the expedition.

He chose Ferdinand Vandeveer Hayden as one of his assistants.[17] Hayden was undoubtedly the most experienced and knowledgeable naturalist and geologist of the western territories at the time, and he had served with Warren in the summers of 1856 and 1857.

Raynolds also chose an experienced topographer, J. Hudson Snowden, who had been with Warren in 1857. Knowing that Bridger, Hayden, and Snowden had all worked with Warren must have reassured Raynolds as he prepared for the expedition.

FIGURE 3. Ferdinand V. Hayden, circa 1865. Courtesy of the U.S. Geological Survey.

Two artists also joined Raynolds' team. One was Anton Schönborn, who had served on the 1856 Warren expedition and whom Raynolds named as the party's meteorologist and chief artist. J. D. Hutton was the party's assistant topographer, assistant artist, and photographer.[18] A number of his photographs were of Native Americans whom the party met along the way. Unfortunately, many of these, along with photos of landscapes, were defective and reflected problems with the new wet plate photographic techniques of the day. Hutton and Schönborn, however, both contributed a number of now-historic drawings along the party's route, including what we believe are the first artistic drawings of the Tetons.

It is important to realize that even though Raynolds was the overall leader of the expedition, the party consisted of two divisions that often went very separate ways. One division was led by Raynolds; the other, by Lieutenant Henry E. Maynadier. While Raynolds was officially the head of both divisions, they often operated at considerable distances from each other. Maynadier's division went on its own route for six weeks in 1859 and for much of 1860. Maynadier's account of his division's work on the expedition is included in Raynolds' *Report*.[19]

One obvious result of this is that when the two divisions were separated, each had only about half the total number of animals, packers, herders, drivers, cooks, and military escorts. Assistants were also split between the two divisions, in which it must be granted that Raynolds usually got the first team and Maynadier got the second.

Overall, the Raynolds party consisted of eight trained assistants, about seven laborers and packers, and an army escort of thirty. The party was very unlike Meriwether Lewis' description of the Lewis and Clark expedition party as a harmonious family ready to work together for a common goal. Instead, the members of the Raynolds party could become cantankerous and rebellious. Raynolds described many of them in his *Report* as

> composed in the main of irresponsible adventurers, who recognized no moral obligation resting upon them. . . . It is thus evident that if gold had been discovered in any considerable quantity the party would have at once disregarded all the authority and entreaties of the officers in charge and have been converted into a band of gold miners.[20]

Raynolds' journal describes how his party did and did not function as it was challenged by daunting terrain and weather—making it not only important history but a compelling adventure story.

A Brief History of the Raynolds Expedition

In addition to a period of almost seven months spent in winter quarters, the expedition's explorations can be divided into three active phases.

Phase 1: April 18 to October 17, 1859

Raynolds received his orders from Captain Humphreys on April 13, 1859. Less than seven weeks later, on May 28, members of the expedition left St. Louis on the Missouri River aboard two steamers owned by P. Chouteau Jr. & Company.[21] Raynolds joined the group in St. Joseph, Missouri, on June 4. By June 13 they reached Fort Randall, on the southern border of what is now South Dakota, where they were joined by the thirty men of their military escort, under the command of Lieutenant Caleb Smith. On June 18 they disembarked at Fort Pierre, near Pierre, South Dakota, where they prepared for their overland trip. Their ten-day stay there included lengthy talks with Indian chiefs whose tribes had been affected by the Harney treaty of 1856.[22]

FIGURE 4. *Four Plains Indian Men, Summer 1859*. Photograph by James Hutton. Yale Collection of Western Americana, Beinecke Rare Book and Manuscript Library.

On June 28, exactly a month after leaving St. Louis, they set off westward on the road that led to Fort Laramie. Two days later, though, they left the road and began to head northwest for Fort Sarpy, which was located on the Yellowstone River about twenty-five miles east of the mouth of the Bighorn River.[23] They traveled over a series of drainages of the Little Missouri River, Pumpkin Creek, the Tongue River, and Rosebud Creek. Delayed somewhat by waiting for boats containing their supplies, they arrived on August 29 at Fort Sarpy. Three months and a day had passed since the party had departed from St. Louis.

Leaving two days later, they reached the Bighorn River on September 2. They passed up the river as far as the Bighorn Canyon and then traveled south on the east side of the Bighorn Mountains, until they turned to the southeast. Having skirted the eastern edge of the basin of the Wind River, they continued on to the valley of the Platte River; and, using the well-traveled Platte River Road, they reached the area near present-day Casper, Wyoming, in mid-October.

From September 2 to October 12, Maynadier's division traveled a different route, exploring the country between the Yellowstone and Platte rivers while following the Rosebud, Tongue, and Powder rivers. On

 FIGURE 5. *Raynolds Party Campsite on the Powder River.* From the chromolithograph of a watercolor painting by Anton Schönborn. From Hayden, *Twelfth Annual Geological Report.*

September 30, Maynadier's group encountered an Arapahoe village of about sixty lodges. The residents of this village were "well-disposed," and a member of the village who spoke English allowed them to obtain valuable information about the remainder of the route. On October 12, Maynadier's division reunited with Raynolds' at the Red Buttes of the Platte River, and they went together to Deer Creek, near present-day Glenrock, and what would become their winter quarters for seven months.

Phase 2: May 10 to July 4, 1860

The period from May 10 to July 4, 1860, is the phase of the expedition featured in this book. Its planned route was relatively straightforward, in the sense that the party was to travel northwest from its winter quarters until it reached the Three Forks of the Missouri River and then turn east to head back toward home. This phase contains that portion of the expedition's route that would have taken the party into the valley of the upper Yellowstone, had it been able to reach this region. Instead, they were forced to go through Jackson Hole, becoming the first governmental party to do so.

On May 10, 1860, the two divisions set out for the junction of the Wind and Popo Agie rivers, near present-day Riverton, Wyoming. Raynolds arrived on May 19, and Maynadier, who had taken a more circuitous southerly route, arrived on May 23. Each division then left on its own route on May 24, planning to meet at the Three Forks of the Missouri River on June 30. Maynadier was to head north on the Bighorn River and then go west, crossing the Yellowstone River before reaching the Three Forks. Raynolds was, in his words, to "ascend the Wind river, and from its head cross to the Three Forks of the Missouri."[24]

While both divisions encountered problems, Raynolds' were the most severe: with all the snow that remained in the mountains, it was impossible to cross from the head of the Wind River through Yellowstone country to the Three Forks. Thus, he would not be able to realize one of the basic objectives of the expedition. Instead, he was forced to lead his division into Jackson Hole, then across the Snake River over Teton Pass and into Pierre's Hole. From there the party headed north until reaching the valley of the Madison River, following it north to the Three Forks.

Phase 3: July 5 to October 4, 1860

The two divisions left the Three Forks on July 5, both heading east for the junction of the Missouri and Yellowstone rivers at Fort Union, "feeling that we were turning our faces homeward." Maynadier would go by way of the Yellowstone, and Raynolds would go along the Missouri. Passing over a series of valleys and ridges, some members of Raynolds' party saw the Great Falls of the Missouri before arriving at Fort Benton on the Missouri on July 14.[25]

At this point, Raynolds split his own division into two parts. One, led by Lieutenant John Mullins, was to proceed to Fort Union by land, following the divide between the Missouri and the Yellowstone. Raynolds and his party would go by boat up the Missouri River. However, the boat that Raynolds had ordered did not arrive, so his portion of the division had to stay at Fort Benton for a week to construct one. They finally left on July 22, and when they arrived at Fort Union on August 7, they saw that Maynadier had already been there several days.[26] Both divisions stayed at Fort Union for a week while a second boat was constructed to transport members of the party and their equipment down the Missouri. Many of the horses, which were broken down by then, were sold.

On August 16, Maynadier led the boats downstream, while Raynolds went by land on a route that largely followed the Missouri. Maynadier reached Fort Pierre on September 2, and Raynolds arrived five days later, having traveled some 2,500 miles since leaving there in May 1859. After stopping at Fort Randall on September 18, they reached Omaha on October 4, at which time the expedition was disbanded. Raynolds apparently finished his preliminary report there immediately after disbanding, since its published version was dated October 5.

Problems Encountered in Mountainous Terrain

Raynolds' division of the expedition encountered a great variety of challenges from the varied terrains they traversed: from arid plains to sagebrush flats, from mosquito-infested meadows to daunting mountains. They faced their greatest tests, however, when they were in the snow-covered Wind River and Gros Ventre ranges near and surrounding Jackson Hole.

Because Raynolds had no prior experience commanding an exploratory party in high mountain terrains, especially in deep snow, he undoubtedly depended on Bridger for advice. Common sense and the experiences of others in his party may also have helped him determine how, where, and when to travel in these difficult areas. The party did use well-worn Indian trails when they could, making traveling considerably easier.

Once the party reached the Wind River Range, Raynolds followed low-lying rivers and creeks when possible. But when fording them became impossible, he and his party were forced to climb steep and rocky inclines; and when these were filled with ice or snow, accidents happened, even the loss of horses and mules.

On the other hand, when the party was in forest areas at lower elevations, they had to make their way over ground that was often strewn with fallen trees and branches—a time-consuming and frequently dangerous process. Measuring mileage became a nagging problem. The party's odometer—a mechanical device that measured mileage by rotation—was mounted on a wagon wheel, then attached by rods to a cart drawn by a horse with a rider. The cart and wheel required constant lifting over log-obstructed trails. The men in charge of the odometer found their work exasperating, and they often reacted angrily to Raynolds when he insisted that they carry out their duties in even the most demanding situations.

Perhaps the most pressing challenge for the party was to find campsites that provided grass for its horses and mules. This, of course, was an even greater challenge when the ground was snow covered. There were times when the party found grass that was not only meager, but barely nourishing. Also, because the animals had to laboriously negotiate high altitude climbs with often-slippery footing, it became important that they be given enough rest to maintain their stamina. As a result, the needs of the party's animals often dictated how, when, and where it traveled, camped, and rested. Raynolds' determination to keep Sunday as a day of rest helped to restore both animals and men. It also provided the opportunity for him to conduct religious services each Sunday morning, although few members of the party attended them.

The Court Martial

Before the party had settled into their winters quarters, Raynolds experienced a sudden challenge to his leadership. It occurred when the party and the military escort reached the Platte Road in October 1859 and began its search for a place to winter. The relationship between Raynolds and Caleb Smith, commander of the escort, abruptly broke apart. Although there were undoubtedly personality differences among the two men, alcohol, easily obtained at way stations along the Platte Road, clearly contributed to the incident, emboldening Smith to defy Raynolds' orders.

Right after the party established a temporary campsite at Red Buttes (just west of today's Casper) on October 11, Raynolds noted that in their return to "civilization," there were some *not* so agreeable signs. Thanks to the ready availability of liquor, many members of the party were in a state of "uproariousness," Raynolds reported, and had "converted the camp into bedlam," requiring great efforts on his part to regain control. To make matters even worse, "the commander of the escort was invisible, and had certainly made no efforts to maintain order or enforce discipline."[27]

Matters came to a head the next day, when Raynolds and Bridger prepared to leave the rest of the party in camp and look for a possible place to spend the winter. They first wanted to investigate the area of Carson's Creek. Smith, however, informed Raynolds that he was taking the entire escort to Carson's Creek and thus would be abandoning the remainder of the party at temporary camp. Raynolds ordered Smith to remain in camp, but Smith replied that he did not recognize Raynolds' orders and would go anyway. When Raynolds and Bridger returned later in the day, they learned that Smith and the escort had, indeed, gone, leaving behind only a corporal and six men from the escort. Maynadier reported that these men were drunk, quarreling, and without provisions and that he had ordered them to join Lieutenant Smith.[28]

On October 14 Smith and the escort returned and encamped again with the party. Smith then offered to consider himself under Raynolds' orders if Raynolds would not report his previous conduct. Raynolds replied that he would consider the matter. Apparently, the more he thought about this the more convinced he became that it was his duty to report Smith's conduct.[29]

Three days later, Raynolds ordered the escort to conclude its duties with the party, to leave with Smith for Fort Laramie, and to report to the commanding officer there. One factor in Raynolds' decision might have been that Smith was once again drunk when he came into camp the previous night.[30]

A week later, after beginning to set up winter residency at Deer Creek, Raynolds wrote Major Day at Fort Laramie about Smith's conduct.[31] Two months later, Raynolds received an order to prefer charges against Smith. On this, as on several other occasions, Raynolds expressed his regret at having to take such an action but saw it as his duty to do so.[32]

In February, Raynolds made a three-day trip of about a hundred miles from Deer Creek to Fort Laramie for the trial. He testified for most of February 17 and was cross-questioned by Smith on February 18 and 20.[33]

Raynolds testified about his orders and instructions on February 24, writing that "[I] now hope that I am through with the court and personally feel no interest in the result." In fact, though, he did care about the result, for he wrote that same evening to Captain Humphreys that he wanted to be informed by the War Department if he was in command of the expedition and, if not, to be "clothed with the authority necessary to give orders to escort."

Smith rested his defense quickly because he had army regulations on his side. The court ruled that, as an engineer, Raynolds was not in a position to command troops; thus, he could not give Smith orders, even though Raynolds was in charge of the expedition and outranked Smith. This decision continued to rankle Raynolds, for he complained about it in his *Report*:

> If the finding in this case is correct, then an engineer officer, in discharge of his legitimate duty, requiring the co-operation of troops, is at the mercy of the line officer, who is not obliged to co-operate with him further than his own inclinations may prompt. . . . The right to order on duty carries with it the right to order in command of the troops required to perform that duty, it being distinctly understood that the duty is such as legitimately pertains to the functions of the engineer officer. Any other construction involves the military absurdity of supposing a junior has the right to thwart the purposes of the officer giving the original order.[34]

Winter Quarters

Aside from Raynolds' brief times at Fort Laramie, he established himself with his party at Deer Creek Station for the next seven months. Near present-day Glenrock, this station had served as a pioneer and Indian trading post, an Indian agency, and a relay terminal for the Overland Stage system. Just four years earlier there were approximately 1,400 Cheyenne, 1,600 Arapaho, and 6,500 Sioux living in the adjacent Upper Platte area.[35]

The station's proximity to the Platte Road—"truly a national thoroughfare," according to Raynolds—meant that supplies and mail were easily available for the expedition team.[36] The party stayed there from October 17, 1859, to May 10, 1860.

Although Raynolds wrote daily entries in his journal during winter camp, he did not include them in his *Report*. Instead, he provided only a

🔙 FIGURE 6. *Deer Creek Trading Post*. Drawing by James Hutton. Yale Collection of
Western Americana, Beinecke Rare Book and Manuscript Library.

brief description of this time in his *Report*, along with an account of the
party's preparations for their upcoming work beginning in May.

Below are portions of Raynolds' descriptions of winter camp that
appear in his *Report*. Raynolds' narrative, made up of his daily journal
entries from May 7 to July 4, 1860, will immediately follow a list of the
personnel on the expedition.[37]

> Deer creek had been selected for our winter residence upon the
> recommendation of Major [T]wiss, the Indian agent for the Upper
> Platte, who is familiar with the whole country, and who had made
> this point the headquarters of the Indian agency. The fact that the
> Mormons had at one time commenced a settlement in the valley
> and commenced to build the houses which we had finished and
> used, also proved it to be one of the best locations in this section
> of the country. . . .[38]
>
> Our log houses, although they had no floors, and only decidedly
> primitive roofs, were still dry and warm.[39] These roofs consisted of
> logs, with brush filling in the interstices, and covered with a coating
> of clay mortar, and above all a foot or more of earth well packed. This
> is the common roof of the plains. A slope of about one foot vertical to
> five horizontal serves to shed the rain perfectly, and the amount that

Winter Quarters. DEER CREEK NEB F V HAYDEN

| α; maj. Twiss' House, | B. Indian-Lodges, Hills, Snow, Ambulance. | Observatory (C) Captains Room (D) Kitchen (E) Computing Room (F) | 2 G. Dining-Room Topograph Room (H) | J Snowden, Fillebrown L Hutton | K. Trooke. Hines, | L. Hayden Schönborn Snow-drift. | 7m. Waring, Huleman Wallace Men's Rooms (0) | n. 7th Maynad ders Room. Atkinson, Stuart. |

FIGURE 7. *Winter Quarters.* Drawing by Anton Schönborn. Smithsonian Institution.

falls is not sufficient to wash off the dirt within one winter, as we fully proved. The winds are in fact much more destructive. . . .

Two or three times during the winter we had snaps of very cold weather, the thermometer in one instance falling to minus 25°. The cold of December 4th, 5th, and 6th was intense, the thermometer ranging from 15 to 25° below zero. On the 6th the wind was terrific, and the air was filled with minute particles of snow and ice, which penetrated every crack and crevice in our buildings.

In my own quarters I had a bank of snow two feet deep that sifted through a crevice of whose existence I was previously unaware. A snow bank also formed on the exterior of our quarters as high as the roof, completely blocking up the doors. It was strange that we did not lose all our animals, but only one was killed, though they had but little or no shelter from the fury of the storm.

Our general occupation was picking up the loose ends of the summer's work, reducing and copying notes, making charts, computing, &c., employment that was both agreeable and profitable.

We were but three and a half miles south of the Platte road, along which the overland mail was carried, and shortly after we were settled the department complied with a request previously made by Major Twiss, and established a post office at the north of the creek,

FIGURE 8. *Our House at Winter Camp.* Drawing by James Hutton, The Huntington Library.

appointing an Indian trader postmaster. We were at once brought within about fifteen days of our friends, the mail coming once a week with such regularity that we could time it within a few hours. The walk to the post office soon became an established event to break the monotony of our life, and after our friends at home learned that we were within accessible distance of their letters, our weekly mail was as large as would be received at a respectable country village.

The pony express was also established while we were in winter quarters, and by it we several times received interesting items of news but three days old. . . .

Not withstanding our mail facilities, our astronomical duties, our map-making, and other official duties, there were many weary hours in winter quarters, when we longed for the social enjoyments of home and civilized life. At times, these were relieved by recounting incidents of adventure in life on the plains which had come to our ears, most of which were heard from the former trappers in this region, some of whom are yet to be found. From all that I hear, I conclude that in the palmy days of the fur trade, before the silk hat was invented, and when the beaver was the great object of attraction, the bands of trappers in the west were little more than bands of white Indians, having their Indian wives, and all the paraphernalia of

Indian life, moving from place to place, as the beaver became scarce, and subsisting like the Indians upon the products of the country.

Bridger says that one time he did not taste bread for 17 years. . . .

One of Bridger's [tall tales] was to this effect: In many parts of the country petrefactions and fossils are very numerous; and as a consequence, it was claimed that in some locality (I was not able to fix it definitely) a large tract of sage is perfectly petrified, with all the leaves and branches in perfect condition, the general appearance of the plain being unlike that of the rest of the country, but all is stone, while the rabbits, sage hens, and other animals usually found in such locations are still there, perfectly petrified and as natural as when they were living; and more wonderful still, these petrified bushes bear the most wonderful fruit—diamonds, rubies, sapphires, emeralds, etc., etc., as large as black walnuts. . . .

I cannot pass over our winter in the mountains without mentioning the prevalent and entire disregard of the laws and regulations in regard to the traffic in ardent spirits in the Indian country. The evening after my party reached Platte Road, at the Red Buttes, liquor was obtained, and many of its members rendered almost uncontrollable. After we were established in winter quarters this continued to be a source of constant trouble, notwithstanding we were immediately under the eye of the Indian agent, and it was only by reminding the traders that I knew the law and should enforce it that I was able to preserve anything like discipline in my command. The sale of liquor in this country is an evil that demands the most effective and persistent remedies.

Early in March preparations were commenced for our summer campaign. I had made requisition for a mounted escort, and knew that it would be necessary to take all our supplies in packs, as it would be impossible for our wagons to accompany us. This involved the purchase of a large number of additional animals and the procuring, either by purchase or manufacture, of pack saddles. A few of these were obtained from the quartermaster at Fort Laramie, but the balance we were compelled to make. Without suitable tools or material this was considerable of an undertaking, but we at last succeeded in producing an article that answered a very good purpose. Indian horses and mules were purchased of the traders, supplies were procured from the commissary at Fort Laramie, and by the first of May we were ready to resume operations.

The fitting out of the pack train with inexperienced packers, extemporized pack saddles, and unbroken Indian horses and mules was, however, a tedious, and at times an amusing, operation. The animals were first loaded with packs of sand to get them used to their burthens, and for a time confined to the limits of the corral. As a general rule they only submitted to the incumbrance after they had been wholly exhausted by the most frantic efforts to free themselves, and I made up my mind that the Indians had sold us only such animals as they could not use, or were too lazy to themselves break for service.

THE RAYNOLDS EXPEDITION PARTY

Leaders:

    Captain William F. Raynolds

    First Lieutenant Henry E. Maynadier

Guide:

    Jim Bridger

Assistants:

    James D. Hutton: topographer and assistant artist

    J. Hudson Snowden: topographer

    H. C. Fillebrown: meteorologist and assistant astronomer

    Anton Schönborn: meteorologist and artist

    Dr. Ferdinand V. Hayden: naturalist, geologist, and surgeon

    Dr. M. C. Hines: surgeon and assistant naturalist

    George Wallace: timekeeper and computer

Assistants in Various Branches:

    W. D. Stuart of Virginia

    J. M. Lee of Virginia

    P. C. Waring of Virginia

    Wainwright Heileman of Virginia

    George H. Trook of the District of Columbia

    J. P. A. Vincent of Illinois

    Calvin G. Wilson of Illinois

    James Stevenson (joined later), born in Kentucky

The Army Escort for This Part of the Expedition:

    Thirty men from the 2nd United States dragoons at Fort Laramie, led by Lieutenant John Mullins

RAYNOLDS' JOURNAL NARRATIVE,
MAY 7–JULY 4, 1860

Monday, May 7

Snowing hard and looking about as wintry as any weather we have had. It is well we have not started.

Tuesday, May 8

Weather better and snow going rapidly. Escort reported about noon.[1] I shall wait a day to let the ground dry and be off Thursday.

Wednesday, May 9

Doing the last of packing up. All busy and yet all seeming to have nothing to do. Maynadier and others went to Bissonett's [*Bissonette's*] and I suspect got more liquor.[2] Finished writing letters at night and now all ready to be off tomorrow.

Thursday, May 10

After nearly seven months in winter quarters we made a start this morning for our summer's campaign. Getting off was more work than I anticipated, but every thing was packed by about 10:30 and we started up the valley of Deer creek over our track into it last fall. Our animals behaved pretty well and but few of them gave any trouble. But the packing had been badly done and many of the packs came off. Our progress was slow but we reached the Platte beyond the "Little Muddy" by 2:20 PM having traveled 11 3/8 miles—much better progress than we made last year. A day or two will I hope enable us to go along finely. We have good reasons to feel well satisfied with our day's march. At the Little Muddy I was charged $10 toll, a great outrage for a road built by Government. Some drops of rain this PM and high wind all day.

Friday, May 11

Our route today was up the Platte road to the "Bridge" which we crossed with the whole train, paying toll of $50.[3] Our train moved along much more smoothly than yesterday tho our packing not yet done as it should be.

From the bridge we passed over the "Sand Hill[s]" a continuation of the same range that is crossed on the route to Powder river from Deer Creek. Descending the hills we encamped on the Platte having traveled 16.08 miles, making it easily in five and a half hours. Grass is anything but plenty and I am now well satisfied that we have begun our trip quite as soon as it was practicable.

The mail over took us at the bridge and brought me a letter from Hall of April 24, the last I shall get probably till I reach Ft. Randall. A mule was killed this morning by breaking her neck while tied up to be packed.

Saturday, May 12

We continued up the Platte Road to the "Red Buttes" where we encamped having traveled 13 miles.[4] The road has been so often described which it is hardly necessary to do so again, but I may say that it could be greatly improved by continuing further up the south side and crossing some five miles above the upper bridge or Mormon crossing.[5] Some of the hills it now passes over are abrupt and difficult, and they could be avoided.

The wind was high from the South West all day which made bad traveling. Towards night it grew very chilly threatening a storm.

Sunday, May 13

I was awakened this morning by some one saying that it was snowing. Looking out of my tent I found the ground white and snow falling rapidly. It continued to fall till about 11 o'clock, and tho it thawed all the time yet at that hour the ground was covered to the depth of four or five inches. The clouds broke away however and before night but little was left in the valley.

The ballance of the escort horses came in about noon having been caught some fifteen miles below. They all looked much the worse for the trip, Lt. Mullin's horse so lame as hardly to be able to get along. He bought two {Indian} ponies to repair damages.

Service at 4:30 o'clock. Read Sermon from Plantation collection from text the "Lord is my Shepherd," etc.[6] Oh that we may all feel how safe we are with such a shepherd to care for us.

Wrote to wife and Hall and Office to Capt. H. [*Humphreys?*] informing him that duplicate notes are at Laramie.

{Our camp is about half a mile up a small stream that flows into the Platte below Red Buttes. The water is brackish, and wood and grass are very scarce.}

Monday, May 14

Cold, disagreeable morning and did not try to get an early start. When we did three horses were missing. The most diligent search failed to find them and we were obliged to go without them. They probably got wandered off after better feed. Lt. Maynadier goes up the {Platte} road from here {to above Independence Rock; thence pass northward to the Popo-Agie and down that stream to its junction with Wind [*river*]} while my route goes up the road some five miles then off to the [right?] over the route we came in on last fall {and join him on Wind river}.[7] We separated in camp, he following me some half hour after. We left the road at the point where it forks to form two roads around the Red Buttes. Thence passing west of a large butte north of the road, we passed once more onto the "plains."

The road was good, our old enemy, the gullies, greeting us at the outset causing one upset of escort wagon, but no other serious delay. We traveled over barren valleys with here and there good grass but no water till we reached the Stream on which we are encamped, having traveled 13.23 miles.

Hunter out but no game. Crossed our route of last fall and now on the same stream we came down.

Tuesday, May 15

Left our camp this morning at 8 AM. Day cloudy but not much wind, far more pleasant than yesterday. We continued on our trail of last year for about 14 miles or to near the point where we encamped Sunday Oct. 9th. The stream which then had water enough in it to supply our camp is more perfectly dry.

We continued on nearly straight diverging to the left of our last year's trail and passing over a rolling divide; encamped on another branch of the same stream we have been following up.

No fuel was to be found excepting sage which answers a pretty good purpose for cooking. The grass is yet scarce, and proves that we have started quite as early as was practicable.

About noon today some Indians were observed a mile or two to our left. Two or three of them came up and proved to be Arapahos who reported Buffalo not far in advance. Numerous tracks and "signs" show that we are coming to them. The Indians said that they had plenty of meat and were now going to a good place to eat it—a pretty good specimen of the providence of the whole Indian community. If the wants of the day are supplied they have no further thought.

We also heard from the Arapahos that the Shoshones were on Wind river and that a small "war party" had gone to the Platte to steal horses of the whites. Stealing horses is making war according to the custom of the Indians—killing is only incidental.

The country passed over today is the same barren desert that we have been in from the Platte, some little grass but no wood or water. I cannot conceive how it ever can be made serviceable to the white man. The whole country between the Big horn mountains to the Platte road is of this character and must be pronounced utterly worthless.

Cleared off at night and I observed, the first opportunity since nearly Red Buttes.

Hunter shot an antelope.

Wednesday, May 16

Left camp at 7:30 AM. Morning clear but cold. Last night was the coldest we have had, at 6 this AM thermometer stood at 24°. By the time we started, however, it was warm enough to go without an over coat. Our route was nearly magnetic west—passing over a succession of spurs many out from the Rattle Snake hills and which gave us a very bad road.[8] In the first six miles we crossed three deep gullies which required much work to get over them. We then struck another that could have required more time to cross than we could devote to it. We therefore turned to the right and passed about a mile down it when by considerable digging a crossing was affected. Resuming our westerly course, passed over gentle slopes to still another branch of the stream emptying {into the Platte} at the "Red Buttes," upon which we encamped having traveled 13.6 miles to effect which we have worked hard for 7 1/2 hours.

The country has been even worse than that passed over yesterday. The gullies [deepen] the hills [*making them*] more barren, most of them indeed having no grass what ever on them. The whole day's march may be said to have been over "bad lands." Most of the hills being washed as bare as a clay bank can be. We are near the western edge of the Valley of Poison Spring creek. We have traveled 48 miles in it and we know that the drainage of this stream covers an area of not far from 800 square miles and yet at its mouth it is nearly dry in the middle of May. Better proof of the barrenness of the country cannot be offered.

Dr. Hayden who was south of the route near the Rattle Snake hills today, reports seeing a band of buffalo and some Indians watching them and waiting for the arrival of the village—one instance at least of the indian herding buffalo.

Wind from the NE this evening and chilly but sky clear and I observed again time and latitude.

Thursday, May 17

About three miles from camp this morning we passed the divide between the Platte and Wind rivers. The road passing over an undulating prairie, so that it was some what difficult to say where the line was crossed. To continue over our course would have carried us into a rough bad land country that would have been difficult to cross and water was very uncertain. We therefore changed our course more to the northward, passing over a gently modulating plain with nothing to impede our progress but the sage {which embarrassed the heavy wagons of the escort}. After traveling 20 1/2 miles we encamped on a small stream of salt water.

The valley in most parts had been burnt over by the indians, but at our camping ground the old grass yet remained. It is dry and worthless however for stock. The soil is in many places covered with a white saline deposit, and some pools of standing water in the valley are so bitter that animals will not touch it.

Some of the hills passed over today had on them a tolerably fair growth of bunch grass, but for the most part they were barren in the extreme. Our last night's camp was on pools of standing water occasioned by the rain melting snow. And, in a twenty mile march, not a drop of water has been seen. Our camp tonight is on salt water that produces rather than quenches thirst and over the whole day's march not a stick has been found big enough to make a "picket pin" and as we have but few of these articles along we find it difficult to fasten our animals. Fuel "grease" wood and "buffalo chips." [9]

The country cannot by any possible means ever be made fit for the habitation of the white man. Indians have been here recently and buffalo "signs" are numerous, but even they have for the present at least, disappeared.

Lt. Mullins is practicing with sextant.

Friday, May 18

Our route this morning was down the valley of Bad Water Creek upon which we had encamped. For some five miles the road was as good as it could be; an even gentle slope, though the soil was rather sticky and in spots wet. Striking over the hills on the south side of the creek we passed some four miles further over a gently flowing prairie and made good progress. We moved on at quite a brisk rate hoping to reach the river, but about 9 miles from camp, hills of close shifting sand came in to the creek on the south side, while on the north, deep gullies crossed the valley at short intervals. Choosing the least of two evils we continued on the south side and plodded our course through the sand. It was hard for even the animals that were ridden and the team mules could barely get along. {The wagon teams made progress with the greatest difficulty.} Fortunately, the creek was close at hand and we could make a camp when ever it became necessary. Continued on till 2 o'clock and encamped having traveled 13 1/2. In the sand hills numerous bands of antelope were feeding and our hunter killed five and other members of the party three. These and rabbits were the only animals seen.

The country passed over was if possible more worthless than that of yesterday. The only redeeming feature being that the water in the creek is not quite as salty as at our last nights camp {though it is still far from palatable}. The grass, too, is better for our animals tonight. The bunch grass in the sand hills, though scarce, is good what there is of it and {our animals prefer it to the} new grass springing up on the flat where we are encamped. It is needed for our animals are not strong and the new grass has not been of much service to them. {The fine American horses of the Escort are suffering most, and it is evident that for hard service they are far surpassed by the tough Indian ponies.}

Saturday, May 19

Our route today was down the valley of Sand Water creek which we were obliged to follow closely. The hills on either side being either loose sand or cut with deep ravines. The water in the creek became less and less as we descended until after passing some eight or ten miles it disappeared entirely, the bed being hard dry sand. Our road crossed the bed continually and was now over sand, causing heavy pulling then through high sage, but it was level and our progress was fair. After traveling some ten miles I ascended a bluff on the south side to take a look for the river. I found the hill cut into deep and impassable ravines and it was with difficulty I reached the summit out of the ravines. I startled three antelope which bounded over the hills too soon for me to get a shot at them. From the summit I could distinguish timber on Wind River which we were obliged to reach to find water.

After traveling 15 miles from camp, the creek circled off to the South and we crossed the bend over a very gradual slope and upon reaching the summit the valley of the Wind River was in full view on our left, only three or four miles off, the valley of Badwater creek to be crossed to reach it. To do this was attended with some difficulty as the best here is a marsh in which some animals came nearly mired. A tolerable crossing was found, however, and we passed on to the river rapidly, descending over a barren clay slope almost to the river rocks projecting near the summit, the slopes covered with a scanty growth of bunch grass.

The upper range of the Big Horn Mountains have been on our route all the way down Badwater creek and when we turned to go to the river the Upper Canõn was in plain sight. When we struck the river the valley was covered with a fair growth of new grass, and we pitched our camp on the edge of a fine grove of young cotton woods (bitter).[10] The first trees we have seen excepting on the distant hills since we left the Platte. The distance traveled being just 100 miles.

Wind River or more properly the Big Horn—for the Popo Agie and Wind River joining should be considered as forming the Big Horn—is here a bold rapid stream. Some what swollen double at present by the melting snow. It is divided by islands into many channels, but where it is together below our camp is about 80 yards in width, four or five deep and the current 3 1/2 or four miles an hour. The water is now muddy and it presents all the characteristics of the Missouri on a small scale.

Distance traveled today 20 miles—the week 100. Our animals need the rest of the Sabbath as the road has been bad and feed poor. Observed at night. Latitude 43° 11 1/2'. {The altitude of our present camp above the sea level is ascertained by barometric measurements to be 4,991 feet.}

One of the Escort horses gave out today.

Sunday, May 20

Day spent in camp as I hope to spend all the Sabbaths on the trip. At 9 o'clock had service, read Mathew 24 and 25 and part of sermon by Mr. Baker from text, "Shame shall be the promotion of fools."[11] I feel that I need faith to conduct these services aright. God grant that I may be able to produce some impressions for good. Service was attended to day by several soldiers and the Waggon Escort. Oh that more would attend and that there might be a general recognition of God's claims to the day.

The weather in this valley has been disagreeable—west wind blowing which is very chilly and uncomfortable making a fire necessary and showing that much snow yet remains in the mountains. This week will probably test our being able to cross them.

Monday, May 21

Started up the river this morning for the mouth of the Popo Agie, the point at which I hope to meet Lt. Maynadier. We had to make something of a circuit keeping on the East side or right bank of the river. The road was over the river bottom and the soil was all as barren as possible—sage being the only product. Between the bunches of sage the ground was bare and consisted of fine white sand, a deposit from the river. Five or six miles from camp, we crossed the only bed of a stream which probably heads in the divide we crossed three days ago (Wind River and Platte), and would probably have given us a more decent route to have traveled. Several low swails [*swales*] crossed the route and near one of them whole acres of ground were covered with a white saline deposit so light as to be raised in a cloud of dust making it disagreeable to pass over it.

A succession of low spurs crossed the latter part of our route. They are tertiary and approaching the "badland" order. Just below the mouth of the Popo Agie an ugly spur of badlands juts out to the river around which it was necessary to make considerable of a detour to pass. From it we descended to the banks of the Popo Agie just above the forks, and crossing it we came into camp in a fine grove of cotton woods with tolerable grass for our animals.

We are much disappointed in not finding Lt. Maynadier here. He has had a better road and tho a somewhat longer route should have reached this point before us. We shall have to wait till he arrives. The Popo Agie where we crossed it is about 60 yards in width, 2 feet deep and current of 4 miles per hour. It is now considerably swollen and is quite as large as Wind river.

I rode up the stream some five miles in the evening to see if I could get any tidings of Lt. Maynadier but did not succeed. Clouds at night and could not observe.

Tuesday, May 22

In camp waiting for the arrival of Lt. Maynadier. Set men to work arranging packs and preparing to go on from here without wagons.

Hunter came in this afternoon and reported seeing eight men on a distant hill. Hope they may be the other party but as a precautionary measure doubled the guard tonight. Sent party up the Popo Agie to look for Lt. M. and to sketch topography and study geology.

Tried to observe at night but haze became so thick that I had to stop after getting a south star and a few observations east. George and self rode up the river some six miles this PM in hope of seeing other party but was of course unsuccessful.

Wrote order for Lt. Mullins to divide escort. Hunter got no game.

{Here I desire to state a fact of some importance with reference to the nomenclature of the Big Horn and its branches. The River which last summer we descended under the name of the Big Horn is formed by the junction of the Popo-Agie and the Wind river at this point, and should properly be called the Big Horn below the site of our present camp. By the trappers, however, it is always spoken of as the Wind river until it enters the cañon some 30 miles below here. There is no good reason for this arbitrary distinction, whereby the same stream passes into the mountains under one name and emerges with another, and it is necessary that these facts should be known to avoid confusion.}

Wednesday, May 23

Sent Pack master and one man to look for trail of persons seen by Hunter yesterday. Returned about two PM reporting Lt. M. and party coming. They arrived about 5 PM having traveled some 25 miles more than ourselves. Hutton caught a mountain trout in Wind river today weighing 2 1/2 pounds {and of the variety so common in the Rocky mountains, the spots being darker than those on trout found in the eastern portion of the continent.} Lt. M. and assistants spent the evening in our camp {making arrangements for our future explorations. We are to separate again at this camp. My own division will ascend Wind river and from its head cross to the Three Forks of the Missouri. Lieutenant Maynadier is to descend the Big Horn to the point at which we left in September, and thence proceed westward along the base of the mountains, crossing the Yellowstone and reaching the Three Forks by Clark's route—the understanding being that we shall meet at the Three Forks on the last day of June.

I deem it important that we should effect a junction by this date at the furthest for the following reasons: On the 18th of July will occur the total eclipse of the sun, which is attracting such attention in all scientific circles.[12] My orders from the department require that, if possible, I should visit the line of the total eclipse in British America (permission having been obtained for this purpose from the authorities of those provinces), and take such observations as may be possible. I propose, therefore, on reaching the Three Forks and meeting Lieutenant Maynadier, to leave the expedition, and with three or four attendants to push on ahead myself to the north, obtaining new horses at Fort Benton, and advancing into the wilderness beyond the international boundary, reaching the eastern base of the mountains north of latitude 52°, just within the line of total eclipse.

The distance from the Three Forks I shall be compelled to traverse will be about 500 miles, and if the two parties shall meet on June 30th, as agreed, I shall have 17 days in which to reach the desired point. As this will require only an average day's march of about 29 miles, I hope to be successful. It will be indispensable, however, that there shall be no delay at the Three Forks.}

Lt. Maynadier and assistants are encamped on the other side of the Popo Agie.

Cloudy night and could not observe which I regret as observations are needed here.

I am now ready to leave in the morning.

Thursday, May 24

Any number of little unthought of things that needed attending to this morning, prevented our getting out of camp before 9 o'clock. Our route was directly up the valley of the Wind river keeping on the South Side and in the valley for the first three or four miles we passed over some fine grass, the valley being a mile or more in width the immediate banks of the stream being covered with a thick growth of cotton wood three or four hundred yards in width.

The Stream its self is larger than the Popo Agie, the bed wider and more cut up by islands and bars. The current is very rapid, the fall being about 10 ft. per mile.

After passing some three or four miles up from the forks, the valley between the bluffs and trees contains little else than sage—and much of it the largest I have yet seen. Many of the bushes being 7 ft. high and four or five inches in diameter at the base. The valley became narrower as we ascended the river and the bluffs so high as entirely to shut out the view of the distant mountains. About ten miles from the forks the river cut the Bluffs on the South Side, and we were obliged either to cross or to go on to the hills. The latter alternative was chosen and we found a succession of gullies that made further bad traveling. After passing about five miles over them, we descended again to the river and encamped on a small point surrounded by the river and bluffs, and only accessible by the route we came in on or from across the river.[13] The grass is only tolerable, but on the hill sides of the ravine through which we came to the river, it is tolerable.

We traveled today 15 1/4 miles in five 1/4 hours over a road that wagons could not have passed in less than double the time. Observed at night and issued order appointing [Lance Corporals?].

Friday, May 25

Ice was found in our buckets last night—showing that it was not without reason that some of us were not able to sleep from cold. {Some of our party spent most of the night around the camp fires, being unable to sleep on account of the cold.} These cold nights and warm days are producing their effect on the party. We have three or four cases of colds or ague or what is called "mountain fever," nothing however that is serious.

A warm sun was shining as we left camp and crossing the river to the north bank continued our journey towards the mountains. The valley was much the same as that passed over yesterday. A bluff on our right presents so fine a point [*that*] to get an idea of the distant topography from that, Mr. Hutton ascended it to get some bearings. Mr. Shonborn [*Schönborn*] accompanied him and having a barometer got an observation. The bluff proved 500 ft. above our camp.

As we ascend the river the mountains approach on both sides making the valley narrower. On the right is the black range of the Big Horn mountains with here and there a snow capped summit—and at places falling off quite low. {One of these latter points Bridger calls "Gray Bull pass," and asserts that through it there is an excellent road into the Big Horn valley.}

On our left is the Snowy ridge of the Wind River range with sharp granite crags projecting as if to defy any attempt to cross them. The valley in which we are traveling presents many imposing views, and the geological features are becoming more marked; as yet we have passed over nothing but the tertiary formation and it extends up to the very base of the mountains.

The soil of the valley is as barren as it can be, perfectly dry and pulverized so that our train raises a cloud of dust that is visible for miles. When we get into camp all who ride in the rear look like so many millers. The appearance of the plain is not unlike that of the sand beach of New Jersey, excepting that the vegetation is not so fresh and green. It was with difficulty that we could find a place to encamp in, and where we are the grass is as hard and dry as in mid summer, little or no new grass being visible.

A strong west wind was blowing all day and coming off the snow in the mountains was quite chilly, so much so that most of the party rode all day with their over coats on.

Some elk were seen in the valley and half a dozen antelope crossed the plain today but our hunter is sick and we got no game. If he is not well in the morning I must send some one else out, as we have not provisions to carry us through without large contributions from the country.

One of my chronometers ran down last night, Mr. Stuart forgetting to wind it up. We traveled to day 20 miles in six and a half hours over roads that wagons could not have passed over at all. Evening hazy and not cold—wind gone down.

Saturday, May 26

Continued our route up the river this morning keeping on the north bank for some 3 miles then crossing to the south. Soon after leaving camp a bear was seen on the opposite side of the river. Bridger had been sick all night and started on the day's trip with reluctance, feeling badly. But the sight of the bear cured him at once. And crawling up to the river's bank he shot across and killed it. Some of the men went across and butchered it and brought the meat into camp. Our hunter, too, was so fortunate as to kill an elk earlier in the day, so that we traveled on with the prospect before us of fresh meat for dinner.

Where we crossed the river it was divided by islands into three channels, the last of which was the only one that was deep enough to make us pick a crossing. Continuing on the South bank we crossed the Lake fork after having traveled nine miles.[14] It is a bold dashing mountain torrent, and when we crossed it I estimated it to be from 1/4 to 1/3 of the whole river. Just above the crossing, it fell some fifteen or twenty feet in a few rods forming most beautiful rapids.

Hutton [*and*] Schönborn went to the bluffs to get a view of "the lakes" and describe them as beautiful mountain ponds about 1/4 a mile a part, the upper about [*blank*] by [*blank*] miles, the lower [*blank*] by [*blank*].[15]

Before reaching the Lake fork a bold drift spur jetted out to the river, and we were obliged to cross it. It is covered with large granite boulders and only a narrow path leading to the top. It was the first serious obstacle our {odometer} cart had met with, but by putting more men to hold it up it was carried up in safety.

On this side of the river we were traveling along a large, well beaten lodge trail and made rapid progress a mile or two further and we had to cross the river again. And tho I had thought 1/4 of the water of the river was contributed by Lake fork, we found this last crossing the most difficult of any.

The current was very rapid, and tho the water was not over three feet deep I was glad when all were across in safety.

After crossing we passed over a wide open bottom covered with salt grass the whole surface of the ground being covered with "alkalie." Striking then across a point of large sage brushes we again reached a timbered bottom with tolerable grass and encamped by the side of a fine spring from which we are supplied with water.[16] The river is only a few rods off, and this evening some of the men have taken quite a number of trout in it. And as our hunter shot a deer just before coming into camp we are now supplied with elk, bear, venizon and mountain trout so the prospect of short allowances is postponed for the present at least.

Clear night and got good observations. Latitude: 43° 19'.

Sunday, May 27

In camp as is my custom on this day. The morning was cloudy and threatening rain. About 2 PM it began falling and has been raining steadily to this time 11 PM. I fear it will raise the river, and as the escort have no tents I fear they will suffer should it turn cold. As yet however it is quite warm.

Church service at 9 AM attended by six of the men and 3 assistants. I am glad to have the men attend as [*illegible word*] that I may be made the means of doing them good. I read that portion of the sermon by Guinness on the prodigal son that dwells on the words, "he came to himself."[17] Oh may many in this camp come to themselves and seek for mercy while yet there is room?

Raining hard as I retire—talked Geo to sleep on reminiscences of Canton.[18]

Monday, May 28

The rain of last night continued till after day light this morning. By the time breakfast was over there appeared some prospect of a clear day and I gave the order to move—as the clouds lifted, the mountains were revealed covered with a coating of snow nearly down to the valley. Every thing in camp was wet and our packing up required more time than usual. We got started at eight o'clock and passing up the valley some two miles crossed the [*Wind*] river to the south side. Our course was about North West and passing over the river bottom presented no obstacles for 10 or 12 miles from camp. We crossed one quite large stream after reaching the river bottom which flowed along it for five miles before emptying into the river. At 11 miles from camp we crossed a second mountain stream.[19] This was a bold mountain torrent flowing over large boulders, and it was with difficulty the mules could pick their way across. After crossing it our road passed round a bluff for half a mile to where the lodge trail we were on crossed the river. On attempting to cross my horse got in so deep that Bridger concluded to try to get along with out crossing. To do so we had to pass for 3/4 of a mile along the side of a steep bluff covered with large boulders—only a bridle path to travel on. By putting ropes on our [*odometer*] cart it was held up for about two thirds of the distance. When not seeing the end I gave the order to abandon it and rode forward to find a camping place. A valley soon appeared but the prospect for grass was bad enough. After passing two miles, a point was situated where the grass was most abundant but at best was poor enough.

After getting into camp and getting dinner I sent back for the cart which arrived before sun down.[20] I walked on about a mile to see the road for tomorrow. We will have to cross the river twice before we travel two miles. We are now getting into mountains in good earnest and the bluffs that come out to the river are almost impassable.

On the south side of the river, where we have been most of the day, the formation is drift, and the chief difficulty is in the large boulders that lie scattered in all directions. On the north side the country is cut into deep ravines, and the tertiary washed or bad land formation stands out in all its naked deformity. The red formation of the "Red Buttes" of the Platte occurs just above our present camp, and all the bluffs on the north side present the peculiar coloring in layers seen on Powder river excepting that the black (lignite) is wanting.[21]

This seems to be a newer deposit and is remarkable so close to the mountains. We have ascended rapidly today having risen some 400 feet where we crossed the last creek. Cedars first crossed our track. The barometer is showing a height of 6,100 ft.

After getting into camp, rain again commenced falling and it is now raining hard. I fear it will be more snow on the mountains and prevent our crossing them.

Distance traveled today 18 1/2 miles.

Tuesday, May 29

Left camp at 7 1/2 AM. Crossed the river after going about a mile. Current is very rapid and water four feet deep. {The recent rains have swollen the stream.} Wind river is more difficult to cross here than near the mouth, the water is higher. By having men stationed in the water to keep the animals headed up stream the crossing was effected in safety. Passed a mile or more of the north side and then re-crossed to the south. These two crossings were made to avoid a bold red bluff that comes out to the river along or around which it was impossible to pass. After traveling four or five miles from camp we reached the "forks" and continued up the south branch before going a mile, it was necessary to cross [*again*].[22] The stream is at present much the larger of the two and flows over a bed filled with large boulders making it very difficult to find a ford. The channel is about 40 yards wide and 3 feet deep. Passed for two miles on the north side then re-crossed to the south making four crossings that we effected in safety in traveling seven miles. Through the whole of this distance the river flows through a gorge with bold rocky banks on one side and sometimes on the other, and it is only by frequent crossing that the train could be got along.

After our last crossing the road continued on the south bank passing over a narrow foot slope of high drift ridges coming down from the mountains, the opposite bank being bold cut bluffs of bad lands presenting the usual horizontal layers of different colors, red predominating. 12 miles from camp we crossed the mouth of a stream that seems to be only the out let of some springs and a small lake at the foot of the mountains.[23] A mile further, we came to a fine brook which Bridger calls "Otter Creek."[24] The grass on it was the finest we had seen and as we had had a pretty bad day I encamped tho we had traveled only 13 miles.

Our Hunter got no game and we are now out of fresh meat. One of our chronometers was injured in some way so as to stop it today.

Observation at night: Latitude 43° 31'.

Wednesday, May 30

Passing over the hills from our camp of last night (on Otter Creek) we descended to the valley of the [*Wind*] river at about a mile distant, continued on the south bank some three miles further, then crossed to the north.[25] The crossing was very much like all we have had. The river seems about as large here as at the mouth. [*We*] had a fine road on the north bank for six miles when we reached a point where it was necessary to cross twice in about 1/4 mile. [T]hen our road continued good with the exception of a single drift spur that had to be crossed, after which we reached the "upper forks" and after making a final crossing continued on some two miles and encamped on the left hand fork at the foot of the mountains.[26] We found the point had been recently occupied by indians as a wintering place, and numerous remains of Lodges and hundreds of lodge poles were on the ground, which Bridger says were thrown away when they crossed the

 FIGURE 9. *Washed Bluffs on Wind River.* From the chromolithograph of a watercolor painting by Anton Schönborn. From Hayden, *Twelfth Annual Geological Report.*

mountains, giving us an idea at least that our tomorrow's work will be difficult, as we hope our next camp will *be on the waters of the Pacific.*

Over all of our route today the Pines and cotton woods occur together on the banks of the river. The Bad Lands disappeared after traveling some 7 or 8 miles, the drift now forming both banks of the river, the boulders from the north being Basaltic and those from the south, Granite.

The view from the spur spoken of was one of the finest we have had, bold craggy rocks (apparently Basaltic) towering above us {to the height of from 3,000 to 5,000 feet} in front and on our right.[27] Smooth pine covered ridges are on the left, the summits of all covered with snow, and the river winding through its narrow valley between presented a picture seldom surpassed. The view down the river was nearly as fine, {a scene whose glories pen cannot adequately describe, and only the brush of a Bierstadt or a Stanley could portray on canvas}.

{Our camp is on the south fork of the stream about two miles above the Upper forks, and at the base of the mountains. From this point we propose crossing the dividing line to the waters of the Pacific. It was my original desire to go from the head of Wind river to the head of the Yellowstone, keeping on the Atlantic slope, thence down the

Yellowstone, passing the lake and across by the Gallatin to the Three Forks of the Missouri.

Bridger said at the outset that this would be impossible, and that it would be necessary to pass over to the head-waters of the Columbia and back again to the Yellowstone. I had not previously believed that crossing the main crest twice would be more easily accomplished than the transit over what was, in effect, only a spur, but the view from our present camp settled the question adversely to my opinion at once. Directly across our [intended] route lies a basaltic ridge, rising not less than 5,000 feet above us, its walls apparently vertical with no visible pass nor even cañon.[28]

On the opposite side of this are the head-waters of the Yellowstone. Bridger remarked triumphantly and forcibly to me upon reaching this spot, "I told you, you could not go through. A bird can't fly over that without taking a supply of grub along." I had no reply to offer, and mentally conceded the accuracy of the information of "the old man of the mountains."}

After dinner, Dr. Hayden and myself started for one of the Peaks that were in front of us, the character of which we were anxious to determine.[29] Passing [*back*] down the fork on which we are encamped we crossed it but not without getting both our horses mired and ourselves in the water.[30] We had become so accustomed to a rocky bottom that we were not expecting this difficulty. On reaching the other fork we found it impossible to cross though the stream was only a few rods wide.

We followed up it for at least six miles and finally got across by finding an old lodge trail. The north or right fork for ten or twelve miles above camp, flows through a marshy valley about a mile in width which at no very distant day was the bed of a lake, and in this valley and in the hills immediately surrounding it the whole stream seems to rise.[31] After getting across we moved rapidly over the hills, passing over the finest grass I have yet seen. Snow was lying in places on all sides and at length we reached the point at which we hoped to get to the crag with ease.[32] It was not more than a mile distant, but between us and it was a deep ravine filled with a thick growth of small Pines.[33] And the day was too far spent for us to attempt to cross it so we were obliged to return with out effecting our object. I felt well paid for the trip however as I got a whole view of the crest of the mountains around the entire head of Wind river—the main chain making a complete semi-circle {forming a natural amphitheater which cannot be excelled}.

FIGURE 10. *Head of Wind River.* Drawing by James Hutton. The Huntington Library.

{Game is certainly abundant in the valley.} While passing in the valley and on the mountain's sides Buffalo "Sign" was so plenty that it confirms the statement that I have heard that the Snake Indians kept them penned in the mountains last winter and killed them as they wanted them. Certain it is that it could be done and a camp where the Indian camp was would do it.

While in the mountains, I saw, as I supposed, a Buffalo feeding in a little valley and cried out to the Doctor to look. He was deceived as well as myself for a moment, but the motions of the beast soon revealed him to be a huge bear. Certainly the largest animal of this species I ever saw. It was only when he moved that the mistake could be discovered, and I was little if any more than 300 yards from him. Having no arms but our revolvers, we concluded it prudent not to get too close.

We also saw several bands of antelope on the hills, one containing 30 or 40 head. Ducks and geese were almost innumerable in the marshes on the banks of the river, so that here at least game seems plenty.

We got back to camp just before a drenching shower, having had a brisk ride of at least twenty miles after our day's march of 14 1/2. {Our camping ground for the night is evidently one much used, as the remains of numerous lodges and hundreds of lodge poles cover the ground.}

Cloudy and could not observe.[34]

Thursday, May 31[35]

Left camp at 7 AM in fine spirits for crossing the continental divide. Our road was directly up a spur of the mountain that came down to our camp.[36] Some of the pitches on it were rather steep, but we got along finely and traveled nearly 3 miles and rose about 1,000 feet in the first hour. Then following the ridge we traveled for three or four miles further through pines and over a pretty good road, when we reached a large wind fall, the dead trees lying in all directions on the side of the hill.[37] It was necessary to pass directly over it, and a good deal of picking the way and some chopping was required. After passing it, the ground rose rapidly and we soon found ourselves in the snow beating it down, and making our way through was hard work. But success crowned our efforts and we reached the last ridge on the Atlantic side. A narrow but deep valley lay between us and the summit.[38] The snow in it was too deep to cross, and the remains of a recent indian camp admonished us at what was coming.

Making a turn to the left to avoid this valley we broke our way for some four miles through the snow, in many places 4 feet deep, the heavy growth of timber compelling us to make a very crooked road.[39] We at length reached the summit of the Rocky Mountains and commenced a rapid descent towards the Pacific [*side*]. Unfortunately for us, we soon struck a valley, the descent of which was not rapid. It was wide and for the most part, covered by snow which was melting rapidly so that the ground when visible was little better than a quagmire. We traveled down it five or six miles when, finding a scanty supply of grass on the southern exposure of the hills, we encamped amid the pines and snow.[40]

The day's march was by far the most laborious we have had since leaving Ft. Pierre. We traveled about 16 miles by the odometer, ascending about 3,000 feet from our camp and reaching an altitude of near 10,000 [*feet*]—descended about 600. Our camp tonight being at an altitude of 9,400 feet.

From the last Atlantic ridge to the summit I preceded the train on foot breaking my way through the snow where it was possible and creeping on all fours where it was too deep. I found the snow in more of a melting mood than I was myself, and I do not know that I ever undertook a more laborious performance or was more exhausted. I had the satisfaction, however, of being the first to reach the summit and of

believing that I prevented the necessity of camping where there would
have been nothing for our animals to eat. Where we are there is little
enough, but the rest, I hope, will enable us to reach better quarters
for tomorrow.

The weather has been such as we may expect while in the
mountains, bright and clear in the morning, two or three snow
and thunder storms through the day and cold and uncomfortable
at night. The moon made an effort to shine and two or three stars
showed themselves near the zenith, but it is not clear enough for
me to observe.

The timber we passed through today is not such as ever to be
of much value, possibly ten trees on an acre would measure a foot in
diameter and might be used if the country was settled, but there was
none that is worth carrying to a market.[41]

Friday, June 1

Did not leave camp this morning till near 9 o'clock as it was
necessary to give the animals all the opportunity possible to graze. Our
course was directly down the valley of Gros Ventre Fork, as Bridger
calls the branch of the Columbia we are on.[42]

{The Gros Ventre Indians have been commonly in the habit of
passing by this valley in their annual trips across the mountains.}
The ground was frozen but not hard enough to bear a horse and the
traveling was about as bad as it could be. About a mile from camp we
came to a small stream not more than 18 inches in width but four feet
deep. It was crossed by bringing the pack animals up to it singly and
making them jump which, as the banks were firm, was not a difficult
thing. Four of the mules refusing to leap, got into the water and had
to be helped out. The valley soon became narrower and the stream
commenced a rapid descent over a rocky bed. Winding our way down
the hill sides, over the rocks and through the mud, we continued some
four miles, when we reached a bold tertiary cut 75 or a 100 feet high
cutting down to the stream, on the slope of which was a narrow bridle
path that our packs passed in safety. But, the recent wet weather had
made the surface too yielding for the [*odometer*] cart to be kept up even
by ropes while the [*illegible word*] attempting it rolled over carrying
mules with it three or four times and landed at the water's
edge and had to be left.

Beyond this point, the path led over a high hill and down to the valley of a small tributary to the Gros Ventre fork where we encamped for the night, having traveled only six miles but having descended 600 feet and passed nearly all of the snow.[43]

The grass was much better than last night but still very far from good, and if we must travel on such poor fare for our animals it can only be done by short marches. Two or three snow storms passed over us during the day tho the sun made an effort to shine at times. Our animals look badly and one of the escort horses and one mule gave out entirely.

After getting into camp we went back for the cart, and by crossing the stream at a pretty deep and rocky ford and making quite a circuit around it, it was got along and is ready to start again tomorrow.

Bridger seems at a little loss to know just which way to get out and rode on after the train stopped to take a look. He reports that it will be necessary to make a short march tomorrow, which I am quite willing to do if we can get to a good place, as rest and grass are both necessary for animals.

Our point of crossing the divide is so much north of where it is placed on the maps that I am very anxious to get observations for latitude.[44] I got out my sextant in the evening when the sky seemed in a measure favorable. But the clouds became too dense for one to succeed. So I have given orders to be called at any hour should it clear off.

Saturday, June 2

The ground was covered with snow this morning, but the sun was shining brightly when the herd was brought up. Before we got started, however, it was again snowing hard. Crossing the stream, which is here about 40 feet in width and 2 1/2 deep, we commenced our march down on the south bank {of the Gros Ventre fork}, the course being north of west.[45] The road was better than any that we have had on this side of the mountains, but snow was falling rapidly and melting about as fast as it fell. Several mud holes had to be crossed but they presented no serious obstruction to our progress. Continued on for about 3 miles when Bridger reported no good camp beyond and in striking distance. I therefore encamped after re-crossing the creek.[46]

The grass is getting better every mile and I hope by the rest of Sunday our animals will be in condition to travel again on Monday. Our object now is to keep as near the summit as possible and re-cross as soon as we can to the head waters of the Yellow Stone.

I have our herd with the guard on the other side of the creek tonight, as I do not think there is much of any danger to be apprehended from indians, and it is worth some risk to get different ground for picketing on the two nights we will be here.

The animal life of this region is quite different from that of the country the other side of the mountains. Even in Wind river valley many birds new to us were collected and Dr. Hayden and Stevenson have been very active. They have got three or four new squirrels, and doubled that number of birds, and today a rabbit that we do not know.[47] Yesterday Bridger shot a mule deer, and the day before our hunter killed one of the same kind near the summit but on the Atlantic waters. The animal is, I believe, not usually found excepting on the Pacific slope.

Tried to get observation of sun but could not, and dense clouds again obscured the sky to night. Thermometer all day was about 40°.

Sunday, June 3

In camp as usual and a welcome day of rest after the toil of the past week. The grass for our animals is better than we have yet had this side of the mountains, 'tho far from what is required. Yet cloudy all day with occasional showers. The sun came out about 3 and I got observations for time. Hoping to get some for Latitude this evening but think clouds will prevent it.

Service as usual. Read 2nd sermon in Plantation series XXIII Psalms, attended only by Dr. H[*ayden*], Stuart, Geo, and Jim Stevenson.[48] May the Lord add his blessing and enable me to persevere in well doing tho I may have little encouragement and not see the fruits of my labors.

Monday, June 4

Our route today was in nearly a NW course—leaving the valley of Gros Ventre fork and striking over the ridges between the branches that flow into it.[49] Our cart left camp after the train with two men to help it along. {A spirit of insubordination and discontent was also manifest among the men.} The men seemed to have got tired of their duty and determined to get rid of the cart if possible. They succeeded in turning it over five times in going about half a mile. I rode back to see what was the matter and by informing them that if I had to leave the cart for such reasons I would leave them, I succeeded in having it brought along.

The road was about as bad as possible. The snow had just left the ground and it was perfectly saturated with water. Every step was through mud and the labor for the animals was excessive. To make long marches is impossible and we will be obliged to move slowly. The best grass is found on the hill tops where the snow has been longest off. In the valleys it is starting finely but is as yet too young to be of much service. I am camped after having traveled only eight miles.[50] Soon after getting into camp, rain commenced falling. Clear fore noons and cloudy evenings and nights seems the order of the day. To night it is raining hard which will give us bad traveling for tomorrow.

Tuesday, June 5

Left camp about 7 1/2 AM, traveled off rapidly to the NW crossing one or two spurs running down towards the Gros Ventre fork.[51] The slopes were not so steep as those passed over yesterday and had it not been for the mud the traveling would have been good. As it was however the animals labored hard sinking in over the fetlock at about every step.[52] The ground is perfectly saturated with water and the loose soil of the mountains make[s] the worst of footing. About 7 miles from camp we crossed quite a large creek and passed up a valley leading down to it.[53] We had traveled about 10 miles when we crossed to the valley of a tributary to the Big fork of Lewis River.[54] Here the mud became almost impassable and occasional patches of snow had to be passed over.

After going some two miles more, the mud became so deep that it was not possible to go on. An attempt was therefore made to leave the open valley to get on to the hill sides and among the pines. Here the snow was lying in large impassable masses with spots of open ground between. The ground was soon found to be even more impassable than the snow, a loose spongy soil in which the pack animals mired at almost every step. Before we had gone [1/4] of a mile we had 25 animals in the mud at the same time that required helping out. To go on was impossible and we were now above the grass so that we could not encamp. I determined to retrace our steps to where our animals could get supplied and to stop till I knew where we were going.

The cart was in the rear today, and on attempting the side hill I sent orders back to abandon it. I was within a mile of the Head of the train and taking it with us on our return. We went another mile back and encamped.[55]

After getting into camp Bridger went onto a high hill to take a look. He did not get into camp until dark and came back with any thing but a favorable report. Snow is visible as far as the eye could reach, yet I do not wish to change our route till I am satisfied it is impossible to go on. I shall therefore remain where we are tomorrow and go on to see if there is any hope of continuing on towards the {upper valley of the} Yellow Stone.

Observed at night. Latitude 43° 40'. It is the first clear sky we have had this side of the mountains.[56]

Wednesday, June 6

Started with Bridger to look at the road ahead {to ascertain if it was possible by some means to cross the mountain range before us, following} up the stream we were on yesterday. We passed up a fork that came in from the left and [formed] a depression in the hills that Bridger said was the "pass." [57] Before reaching the fork we found much difficulty in picking our way around snowdrifts and through the mud. After leaving the main stream the ground rose rapidly and the hill sides were covered with a dense growth of {stunted} pines, under which the snow was lying in all directions. Some of the banks our horses could plunge through, but many of them had to be trodden down before we could pass them. The labor was severe in the extreme. But by perseverance we finally reached the summit. As soon as we had done so, Bridger pronounced the "pass" the wrong one—the drainage on the other side running off too much to the South.[58] {We had expended our efforts in climbing a spur.} We therefore descended and went up the main stream. This carried us up more to the eastward and on starting up did not look as favorable as the other. By following in the bed of the creek for some distance and breaking our way through snow banks, we succeeded in going perhaps a mile.[59] There the stream ran through a comparably wide valley about 3/4 of a mile in length. Steep cliffs cut by deep gorges came down on all sides.

The whole valley was covered with snow, and all the gorges and hill sides were filled {to a uniform depth of from eighteen inches to two feet, without the slightest appearance of ever having been crossed by man or beast}. Before reaching this point I had not only walked but led my horse over spots of hard packed snow. Bridger said this was "the Pass," but we, as well as our horses, were too much exhausted to go further. We had been wading through snow drifts all day and were as wet as though they had been water. We therefore returned determined to make another attempt tomorrow. Hard rain tonight which will make the snow worse.

Thursday, June 7

Started this morning with a party of nine, all told, to make a final attempt to get through the "Pass." Bridger, Mr. Hutton, Dr. Hayden, Mr. Schönborn, myself and 4 men. While going up the creek the mule on which one of the men was riding fell down and came near drowning.[60] He was sent back to camp {with rider}.

The rest of the party reached the point where we turned back yesterday by following our track without difficulty. Then came the "Tug." The snow in the gorges compelled us to take the valley. Here the stream was flowing in a very circuitous channel from side to side. It was from three to four feet in width and from 2 to six feet in depth, flowing between muddy banks about two feet below the surface. The whole valley was a uniform surface of snow and water.[61] After considerable trouble we got down to it. The snow was not so deep but that it could be broken through almost any where. But we soon found that there were innumerable side gullies moving into the stream that were not visible under the snow {into which we tumbled, and out of which we floundered in a style at once ridiculous and exhausting} and that at every step we were liable to sink up to the waist. After having done so often enough to get experience, the ground was tested with a rod at every step and by following the windings of the creek and frequent turns to go around gullies, and occasional climbs over bluffs where the creek cut them, the upper end of the valley was at length reached. Here the creek was found to come down through a narrow gorge on the sides of which the snow was banked up from 40 to 50 ft. in height. I concluded it was useless to make a path further for animals without knowing what we were to have on the other side. So leaving our horses, Mr. Hutton and myself, with the men, went on to the summit. We passed easily over the surface of most of the snow banks, and at length looked down upon the country beyond the ridge.

As far as the eye could see nothing but deep gorges, pines and snow were to be seen. The prospect ahead was far worse than what we had passed over. To get our train to this point would be next to impossible. But it would be attempted if there were any hopes of {getting through the snow on the Yellowstone side of the mountains}. To go on can be nothing but certain loss of our animals if not of ourselves. I therefore reluctantly concluded to abandon this route and tomorrow start for a more western pass onto the Head of the Madison. I fear the passage of the 3 Tetons range, but this or going back by Wind river is the only thing left.

{After taking in our fill of the disheartening view we returned to camp, to commence the execution of our new project on the morrow.}

Our Hunter brought in two deer to day which helps out our supply of provisions.

Occasional showers today but clear and cold tonight.

Friday, June 8

Started reluctantly this morning to try another route to the waters of the Missouri, retracing our steps for some 3 miles. We passed down one of the branches of the Gros Ventre fork to its mouth, thence down to near the Indian trail from Green River.[62] Our herd had to be sent too far from camp to get grass for us to get an early start, and the first part of the road was very muddy so that our progress was slow.

After leaving our old trail we passed along the brow of the hills bordering the stream, and tho the Pines and cross ravines interfered somewhat with our progress, we got along better than we could have done in the valley. Just before reaching the Indian Trail, we passed over a pretty steep spur and came down to the valley of another stream (the one I think we ascended yesterday to its source) and encamped in fine grass {near its junction with the Gros Ventre}.[63] Crossing this spur was useless labor, but Bridger mistook this point which is no very wonderful thing as he has not been in the country for fifteen years. His general knowledge is fine, though in the details he makes frequent mistakes.

The change in the appearance of the country in our short march of 12 miles today has been marked. For three days past we have been just on the limits of passable grass for our stock, but every step today made it better, and tonight we are in as good as any we have seen. This morning, evergreens alone were visible. Now we are among cotton woods. These willows are larger, flowers more abundant and every thing indicates a lower and more productive country. The soil is good and needs only *warmth to produce well.*

The weather still keeps up its reputation for variableness. About noon we had a heavy fall of rain, snow and hail, attended with vivid lightning and heavy peels of thunder. The mountains behind us are shrouded in thick black clouds, while the sun was shining brightly on the snowy summits of those in front, the whole forming a scene decidedly more romantic than agreeable.

Saturday, June 9

Left camp at an early hour this morning, hoping to make a long march. Raising the hill to pass over to the main stream the view that presented itself was exceedingly fine. The valley of the stream stretched out before us clothed in green, bold Mountains bordering it on either side covered with dark evergreens and snow. In the distance a craggy red cliff seemed to cross the valley while rising behind it and in the centre of the section was the high snow clad crags of the great Teton {dazzling in the clear atmosphere with the reflected rays of the newly risen sun}. As the view burst upon us there was a simultaneous exclamation and admiration {and the accompanying sketch fails to do justice to the scene, the artist confessing his inability to represent the glorious coloring}.[64]

Our route was directly down this valley, and the train moved on rapidly for about five miles, when it became necessary either to cross the stream or pass over the hills. The water, tho not very deep, was so very rapid that the latter course was adopted. Two high spurs had to be passed but by taking advantage of ravines they were both passed without any steep pitches. While in advance of the train, word was brought me that a dragoon horse had slipped and got badly snagged. Returning I found him bleeding profusely. The snag had entered well up in the inner part of the hind leg and doubtless had cut a vein. The flow of blood was checked by the use of cotton and sewing up the wound. And, as it was impossible to bring him on, he was left to be sent for tomorrow.

We reached the river just above the red bluff seen this morning.[65] To get around it, it was necessary to pass close to the edge of the water, along a narrow foot path under a high precipice. Three mules pushed on, passed the drivers and got so high up among the rocks that the men would not follow them on foot. Two succeeded in getting down again in safety, but the third lost his footing and fell over a sheer precipice, near fifty feet in height, then rolled into the river and swam

FIGURE 11. *Great Teton from Pass No Pass.* Drawing by James Hutton. Yale Collection of Western Americana, Beinecke Rare Book and Manuscript Library.

across. His packs came off, part on the hillside, part in the river, and one bundle he dragged out with him. I {immediately ordered the party to encamp} and set to work to repair damages. One of the men succeeded in getting across the river. The mule was dead. Two bundles of bedding were on the other side. The current was too swift to attempt to bring them back by any ordinary means so a rope was got across by first throwing a stone with small twine attached, and in this way the beds were got back, wet, but not other wise injured.

The stream here is 30 yards wide, about 4 ft. deep and current five or six miles an hour. The whole stream would be rapids any place else. A horse with his pack was missing on arrival in camp this evening. We have a variety in our mishaps for the day, but I hope he and the dragoon horse will be brought in tomorrow. Cloudy at night and could not observe. Distance today 15 miles, course West.

Sunday, June 10

Another welcome Sabbath. Service at 9 AM. Read part of sermon from text "I, even I, am he that blotteth out thy transgressions for mine own sake." [66] Attended by the usual persons and two soldiers. May God add his blessing.

 FIGURE 12. *The Tetons Looking Down Gros Ventre Fork.* From the chromolithograph of a watercolor painting by Anton Schönborn. From Hayden, *Twelfth Annual Geological Report.*

Sent for dragoon horse and missing packhorse. Both came in about 2 PM. I hope the horse may yet be able to do duty. [*Our*] hunter went out and brought in a deer which was necessary as our supply of provisions must be husbanded. Day very changeable with sunshine, {snow} and rain about every alternate half hour.

Clear at night and I attempted to observe. Got East star but clouds obscured the sky before I got through with the North and compelled me to stop.

Monday, June 11

Continued our route down the Gros Ventre fork. We are now on the regular Indian trail and the traveling is good tho the road is hilly for the first seven miles, as it passes over the spurs leading down to the river, there being no river bottom.[67]

After traveling about 7 miles we reached the brow of a hill and looked down upon "Jackson's hole."[68] It is a wide level valley extending up the river apparently to the foot of the main chain of Mountains and is bounded on the West by the Teton range, the east by the high spurs we have been traveling over. {Its approximate area is 100 square miles.} After the rugged Peaks we have been seeing for weeks just the sight was delightful. Snake River flows close to the Mountains on the West side of the valley, and we turned to the left crossing the Gros Ventre and continued our course so as, if possible, to reach the river at a point at which it might be forded, Bridger insisting it could not be done above. A bold butte standing just below the mouth of the fork had to be crossed before we reached the river, upon the banks of which we encamped having traveled twenty-five and 1/2 miles {the extraordinary distance being explained by the excellence of the road and the weather}.[69]

Passing through Jackson's hole the traveling was so fine that no one realized how far we were going. The scene too helped to wile away the time. A small variety of Sun flower was in full bloom and covered large portions of the valley with their golden flowers which, in contrast with the green of the rest of the valley and the hill sides and the snow clad summits of the Mountains, presented a picture not easily forgotten.[70]

While passing through the hills soon after leaving camp, word was brought forward to me by Mr. Hutton that a small band of Indians were seen by himself and others watching our movements. As they ran when approached we conclude them to be a band of Blackfeet. And as they know they have been discovered and probably see us about as much as we do them, I only halted long enough to close up the train and move on. But to prevent their taking our animals, I have tonight doubled the guard.

As soon as we reached the river a search was made for a ford, but the prospect seems bad enough. The river is here divided into an almost innumerable number of channels and flows with the rapidity of a torrent. Some indians were encamped on the opposite bank who saw some of the party and came over to see us, swimming their horses to do so. They are a small band of Snakes—and seem as harmless as people can be. They were a good deal surprised when we told them we had seen other indians during the day and at once confirmed our suspicions of their being Blackfeet. They returned to their lodges after staying a very short time and begging a few plugs of tobacco.

Several hard showers today as usual.

Tuesday, June 12

Moved camp this morning down the river about two and a half miles to the indian crossing in hopes that we could make it available. As soon as we got into camp, Lance Corporal Lovett started to look at the ford. Seeing him starting I told him to go on as far as he could and let me know how it was. A few minutes after, I saw Lance Corporal Bradley following him. Within twenty minutes after, Lovett came back hollering that Bradley was drowned. All hands started at once to the rescue, but the deep channels and thick growth of brush prevented making any progress and, as soon as it was known that he had gone down in one of the swiftest currents, all hopes of saving him were abandoned. I however started parties to look for the body and the indians coming into camp soon after started them by promising reward {for its recovery}. The river was carefully examined before the search was abandoned, but all is vain. {The calamity is deplorable, but it is one of those sad accidents for which blame attaches to no one.}

Other parties were out in the mean time looking for a crossing, and about noon word was brought that a point had been found at which it was thought possibly a raft might be used. Some of the men were set to work under Mr. Hutton to construct the raft {and completed it late in the afternoon. We shall try the experiment with it tomorrow}. Taking one man with me, I went to examine the river above. I wanted to look particularly above the mouth of the stream we had come down, which in commemoration of the sad event of the day I have concluded to call "Bradley's fork."

I passed up the river bottom some eight miles and found it to be some forty feet below the plain over which we traveled yesterday, and every where to consist of a black vegetable mold through which it would be next to impossible at this stage of the water to pass a train— to say nothing of the difficulty of crossing the river with such a bottom. I therefore returned to camp after having traveled some 30 miles in vain and determined to try the raft, which I found done, tomorrow.[71] It rained hard again while I was out this after noon.

The river has now been examined over a distance of about 25 miles for a ford but without success.

Wednesday, June 13

Moved about half a mile so as to be near the point to take the raft. Stopped the train on the edge of the timber and took men over to first try the raft. The current was too rapid to turn it adrift, and on attempting to send it over, having it checked by a rope to shore, it [behaved] itself so badly that this plan had to be abandoned.

Before starting out I brought Bridger's talent into play by setting him to work with all the spare men to make a boat. When I returned I found they had made good progress and I ordered the train into camp where we were and set all hands to work to finish it. Our great difficulty is a covering. We have no skins, and I am compelled to use the Gutta Percha blankets bought of Mr. John River of N.Y. which like the tent, knapsacks, and all the articles purchased of him are so rotten as to be next to worthless.[72] To protect it I am going to use a lodge skin that Bridger has, and have had every body I could spare, out gathering resin from the pine trees so as to prevent this from absorbing water. We have got a pretty fair looking boat nearly finished about 12 1/2 feet long and [*with a*] 3 1/2 [*foot*] beam. {It is remarkable for the fact that it is constructed entirely without nails or spikes, the framework being bound together with leather thongs.} If we can make our covering answer I hope, Providence permitting, to get across in time.

Three channels about 100 yards in width have to be crossed. Two of which a loaded horse can swim, and the 3rd is too deep and swift to swim between these channels. Unless we can find a better point the goods must be carried by hand. Some more indians visited us to whom I made a small present. This is the first day we have been on this side of the Mountains without rain.

Thursday, June 14

Our boat was ready to be launched about 9 AM. It then had to be carried over the Sloughs and Islands near a mile to the point of starting, putting 4 of our best swimmers in it and a small load of Indian goods.[73]

The first channel was crossed in safety. Search was then made for a crossing beyond and a point situated at which the two remaining channels could be crossed at once. The goods and boat had to be packed by the 4 men. But the main shore was at length reached in safety and the boat packed to a point above from which the three channels could be avoided and the crossing made at once. After seeing the boat start on her return trip, I came back to camp. The men got in about 5 PM, too late to do any thing more this evening than to prepare for an early start tomorrow.

Our boat requires three men to manage her in this rapid current, which will only permit us to carry very small loads, so that time will be required. {I regret the delay but it is unavoidable.} The river is rising which will give us additional trouble.

Friday, June 15

Commenced by 5 AM to make our crossing. The goods had to be packed across Sloughs and Islands over a mile from camp, then put into the boat and loaded 1/4 of a mile (by measurement) below the point of starting. The boat was then carried 700 paces upstream and then crossed to a point 200 paces below the point of departure. After carrying it over this space, it was ready for another load. Men were stationed to catch her and do the carrying and after getting all at their posts the round trip was accomplished in 3/4 of an hour. The current is too swift to attempt sending anything over on the animals and all must be carried in the boat, even to halters and picket ropes.

The boat has made 17 trips today. But much still remains on the other shore. I crossed early in the day. Every thing is now on the beach ready for boating and two or three unsuccessful efforts have been made to cross the herd. The moment they strike the swift current they pull back, and no effort has succeeded as yet in making them swim across, and no one is willing to venture to lead them. The Sergeant with the guard have them in charge tonight. 15 persons all told are yet on the other shore and at least another day will be required to get all across.

Saturday, June 16

The men who were in the boat yesterday are so sore and sun burnt (having worked all day ready to swim at any trip) as hardly to be able to go to work this morning. They did not hold back however and I started them off with orders to cross the herd first. Lance Corporal Lovett volunteered to lead the way. The animals were now divided into 2 bands and [expertly] taken to where the first attempt was made with the boat, and where the river is divided into 3 channels. After much trouble the first band was finally made to follow Corporal Lovett, and got ashore in safety. And the second band also got across without accident, 'tho some of the animals swam and drifted a mile down stream. The men who had driven them to the crossing had now to be taken off with the boat after which she commenced her regular trips and brought over 10 more loads, landing everything on this shore but the cart which I have concluded to abandon as it is running too much of a risk to attempt to bring it.

Our things are badly scattered on the shore and some time will be required to gather them together. But I feel that we have been specially blessed to have gotten over without accident. The main channel at this point is about 100 yards. Yet, as I have said the boat drifted 1/4 a mile in crossing, and not withstanding an eddy about midway which was taken advantage of to paddle up and across stream, the distance between landings was passed over in 2 minutes. This makes the current a full 7 miles per hour.[74]

Sunday, June 17

A welcome day of rest after the labors of the past two days. Mr. Alexander {my foreman} volunteered to go for the cart, which he attempted to tow on a raft but had to abandon it in the stream. Much of the day was consumed in getting packs together and ready for starting tomorrow.

Service at 9 PM, attended only by Dr. Hayden and George. Did not read a Sermon. Cut Nose, whom Bridger says is the hereditary chief of the Snakes, was in camp all day [*and I*] made him a small present.

Some Indians brought some fine trout to camp that were bought by some of the men. I tried to buy for all the party but could not. Day warm and musquitoes very numerous. Yesterday a light snow storm. Changes enough surely to satisfy any one.

{Our camp is now on the right or west bank of the Lewis or Snake river and about 10 miles southeast of the highest of the Tetons, the most noted landmarks in this region. They are basaltic peaks, rising not less than 5,000 feet above the level plain of Jackson's Hole, and are visible from a great distance from all directions.[75]

Our route out of this valley will be to the westward and across the mountain chain of which they form a part, and which forms the western boundary of the valley we are now in.}

Monday, June 18

Some of our animals having strayed, prevented our getting an early start this morning. We were out of camp a little before eight and passed directly west to the mountain, crossing a fine stream about 1 1/2 miles from camp. The ascent of the mountain is effected by taking advantage in the valley of a stream flowing down its side, and our road most of the way up was along a bridle path through the pines with the dashing mountain torrent below us, and the steep mountain side above. The path is quite steep towards the summit but not bad for a pack train. Large snow banks were passed before reaching the summit, but nothing to interrupt our progress until we descended the Western Slope. Here we found the snow so deep as to compel us to leave the indian trail and climb the spur, some two or three hundred feet higher, and then to seek out a path along the mountain side 'till we got below the snow. It was a difficult undertaking and part of our route was so steep that those who were in advance were in great danger from the stones started by those in the rear. It may be that when the snow is gone this pass is a good one for packs, but at present the most that can [be] said is we passed over it.[76] The summit is about 7 miles from the river and 1900 feet above it. 1000 feet was descended in not over 2 miles on the west side. A pine tree by the side of the path and on the summit was marked JM July 7th 1832 and July 11, 1833.[77]

After the first two miles from the summit the descent was in the valley of a small stream and more gradual. And passing down for some 8 or 9 miles we encamped on the edge of Pierre's Hole having traveled by estimate 18 miles. Some fine pines were passed today, a few as much as 4 feet in Diameter. But, by far the greater part is fit only for tellegraph poles.

Tuesday, June 19

Our course today was nearly north passing down through Pierre's Hole which almost deserves the praise bestowed upon it by Bridger, who says it is the finest valley in the world.[78] It is some 7 or 8 miles in width and 20 or 25 miles long, bounded on all sides by snow capped mountains, watered by a fine stream through the middle and four or five smaller branches flowing down from the Mountain, very slightly undulating and covered with a luxuriant growth of grass and all most innumerable flowers of which the small variety of Sun flower predominates, spreading out a golden carpet as far as the eye can reach. The banks of the stream were some what muddy and required care in crossing.[79] One caused considerable delay. But the train moved on rapidly and we were in camp by one o'clock, having traveled between 17 and 18 miles.

The Tetons showed out finely on our route today, forming a prominent land mark. And in front and to the left of our course is a high snow clad mountain which Bridger says is at the Head of the middle fork of the Jefferson. We are now aiming for the Head of the Madison and as far as the eye can see, nothing is in the way to interrupt our progress.[80]

Tho this valley is so fine and the grass so plentiful, it is destitute of game. Not a quadruped larger than a squirrel has been seen today. Even the birds are scarce, a few curlew and some smaller birds being the only ones seen. We need game as our supply of provisions is limited and I trust we will soon get where we will find it.

Wednesday, June 20

Leaving the valley of Pierre's Hole we continued our course to the northward and passing over an open rolling country the hills from 100 to 200 ft. in height with occasional steep sides leading to the beds of streams. These streams are all swollen at this time and all cause more or less delay to find a crossing. The hills have at no distant day been covered with aspens as the decaying trunks testify. The soil on all of them is good, and a fine growth of grass is found almost every where.

Passed a fine stream and good camping ground at one o'clock, and as I am anxious to get along as rapidly as possible concluded to continue our march an hour or two longer. Rising the hill beyond, we soon came to a thick growth of young pines and aspens—among which the dead timber was lying in all directions.

Picking our way through the brush in advance of the train, Bridger and myself soon began a steep descent to the Valley of a large stream which, as soon as he saw it through the thicket, Bridger pronounced to be Henry's Fork.[81] He had mistaken his locality and was more surprised to find {this formidable river} than any one else.

To take the train down where we were was impossible and we knew nothing of the state of the river—so I sent back to have the train return to the stream we had crossed and go into camp, while I went on with the Guide to find a crossing.

Leading our horses down the hill we reached the river bank. It was flowing between deep banks very rapid and apparently too deep to ford. We then passed down the river and tried it at several points, but with out success. I at length left Bridger to go on down while I returned to cross the hills to camp to set men at work to build a boat. All the trees [required?] were found and chopped into shape before night and ready to take with us to the river in the morning.

As soon as I got into camp I sent the Packmaster and one man to make further search for a ford. They returned at night—but found no place where it was practicable. Bridger returned having found a good place for boating with good camping ground on both {banks}.

A [*illegible word*] hail storm passed over camp this after noon, accompanied with a gust of wind that blew down our tents and gave us a slight drenching, but caused much more inconvenience by changing the air to any thing but an agreeable temperature.

Thursday, June 21

(Day cold enough for overcoats all day.)

We were taking our breakfast this morning when the sun rose. Being anxious to get an early start to get to the river and across, we were on its bank at 7 AM and had traveled about 3 miles. Commenced at once to put our boat together and had got about half done, when one of the men who I had sent to continue the search for a ford found one below where we were that was practicable for the larger animals. I had the herd at once driven in, and selecting our largest animals and making two trips with them, landed every thing across the river in safety.

The day was so far spent that I would not go on, especially as Bridger wanted to look ahead. He started as soon as he got across and returned before night, reporting some thick pines to be passed through but other things favorable. Our stock is in good condition for traveling and I still hope by a little hard traveling {to fulfill my engagement with Lieutenant Maynadier} and to reach the 3 forks by the last of the month.

Friday, June 22

Left the right bank of Henry's fork and passed directly over the Hills towards the northward and our course being about NNW.

The country passed over was very much the same as that yesterday, with the addition of pines and aspens growing in many places so thick as to be almost impossible to get along. I had a pioneer party in advance with axes to clear the way and blaze the road. In many places the young pines are growing between the fallen trunks of their predecessors, and we passed for miles over ground where I was constantly expecting to hear that some of our animals had been snagged with two or three not very serious scratches. However, all came through in safety.

One quite large stream was passed which Bridger mistook for the Spring fork. Crossing it and continuing our route over the hills through the pines we reached a second stream about 40 yards wide and a foot in depth flowing with a gentle current over a gravel bottom that he said was the Lake fork—but added, "I thought the Lake fork was bigger."

The valley was narrow but we concluded to try to go up it rather than keep in the timber. After traveling some 3 miles we came to the "Spring" {showing that Bridger had been mistaken, and that this was Spring fork}. Here was the feature not to be mistaken—and our guide knew at once where he was. Fully two thirds of the stream came from the side of the hills breaking forth about thirty feet above the stream, making as fine a water fall as can be found. It is by far the largest spring of which I have any knowledge, and once seen would not be easily forgotten {and is famous all through this region}.[82]

We continued up the small branch above the Spring for two or three miles further, when the valley became too narrow to follow it further. So passing out of it, we came to an open marshy spot in the pines that furnished grass of a poor quality where we encamped for the night. The musquitoes being so numerous as to be any thing but pleasant. As night approached however they ceased their songs and permitted us to pass the night comfortably. This morning we had ice a quarter of an inch thick in our buckets, which it would seem should have prevented our being troubled with musquitoes this PM. Our hunter brought in the meat of a bear he had killed this afternoon, which is very acceptable as we have had no fresh meat now for nearly a week.

The Camas plant is growing in large quantities in the swamp near camp. We have had some gathered and cooked. Bear meat and camas are two important additions to our supplies.

The Camas is a bulbous plant bearing a beautiful blue flower. The bulbs there are from 1/2 an inch to an inch in diameter. These only are eaten. They are not unlike onions without the peculiar flavor and seem to contain a large proportion of gelatinous {glutinous} matter.

Commet visible to night.

Saturday, June 23

Started this morning determined if possible to get out of the woods. Our route was over quite level ground between the Spring and Lake forks of Henry's river. Thick small pines, sharp basaltic rocks, thick fallen timber or wet marshy ground were in our path by turns during all the first half of our days march—and not infrequently two or even all of them combined to prevent our progress. Picking our way along as best we could, at times taking advantage of a deserted indian trail which assisted materially, we at length opened into a long level prairie of hard basaltic gravel, over which we passed rapidly for more than hour when we again reached the pines. Near the end of this prairie, we passed two quite large tributaries of the lake fork. They were flowing on the surface and spreading out over the level prairie, [and] made a large part of it wet. And the cloud of musquitoes over them rendered men and animals almost frantic. After some search "the trail" was again found and we succeeded in following it for most of the way through the pines which continued until we reached the right bank in an open span some 10 feet above the water.

The Lake fork is here about 100 yards wide and 3 ft. deep, and current 2 miles per hour.

Game again came in sight today. We have gotten two deer and an antelope, and two herds of 30 or 40 each of Elk have been seen, so that our prospect for fresh meat is much better than it has been. We are now, Bridger says, through the timber and I hope nothing further will delay our progress to 3 forks.

Latitude tonight is 44° 30'—some 25 miles N of where the divide is down on the maps.[83]

Sunday, June 24

In camp as usual on the Sabbath. Service at 8 AM attended only by Dr. Hayden, Mr. Stuart and Geo. God grant me grace to continue my feeble efforts to do good, notwithstanding I may see no fruits, and tho but few seem to take an interest in them.

The day commenced warm and pleasant and I had service early to avoid musquitoes. Day continued pleasant till after dinner when it commenced raining and continued all after noon—and became much cooler.

Monday, June 25

Started this morning in a NE direction through a strip of woods which continued about a mile, when we emerged upon an open and nearly level prairie which continued to Henry's lake. The first mile or two was quite wet but the ballance of the way good firm traveling. About 10 miles from camp we crossed the lake fork which is here a rapid stream, flowing between muddy banks, and about 25 yards wide and 3 ft. deep. We then passed around the east side of the Lake—being obliged to keep out some distance, to avoid swamp[s], and along the foot slopes of the mountains. The Lake is from 3 to 4 miles long, and after passing it we commenced a very gradual uniform slope to the

"Pass" which is 4 miles above the lake. As we approach the summit I put spurs to my horse and galloped into Nebraska (driving a herd of antelope before me).[84]

The summit is only about 200 ft. above the lake and is so flat that it is some what difficult to tell the exact point where the waters divide. From Mountain to Mountain it is about a mile in width, and the sides slope gently down to the centre. In the pass the barometer stood at 23.65 inches which indicates a height of about 6350 ft. {above the sea level}, or more than 1500 ft. below the South pass.[85] The approach to it from either side cannot be surpassed, as it is a uniform gradual slope of about 50 ft. to the mile. It well deserves the name I have given it of the "Low Pass" and presents every facility for either wagon or Rail Road purposes. {I deem it to be one of the most remarkable and important features of the topography of the Rocky Mountains.}[86]

From the pass we continued on some 10 miles and encamped on the bank of the Madison below the cañon. The Madison here is about 80 yards wide flowing with a rapid current over a bed filled with large boulders. It looked too formidable for us to attempt to cross it.

Our whole route today, with the exception of the marsh I have spoken of, has been over fine ground for traveling. All the way we have passed over a most luxuriant growth of grass—and large bands of antelope have been scattered over the country on all sides of us. Our progress has been rapid and by observation I find we have made 20' of northing.

After crossing the Lake fork, Mr. Hutton, Dr. Hayden, Geo and Jim went to take a look at the pass {leading} into the "burnt hole" {valley}.[87] They found {the summit distant only} about 5 miles to the right of our route, and report it as in every respect equal to the Low Pass, and that they could see {a second pass upon the other side of the valley, which Bridger states to lead to the Gallatin}.

From there according to Bridger no mountains have to be crossed to reach the Yellow Stone, and if so this would be the shortest and best route for a rail road. After crossing the Lake fork the route is clear over Camas Prairie and on down Lewis fork.

I have little doubt that it is the true pass for a road across the Rocky Mountains.

We came near having a serious accident on the road to day. The carbine of one of the escort went off while lying across his saddle and

≈ FIGURE 13. *Henry's Lake and the Tetons from the Summit of Low Pass Looking South.* From the chromolithograph of a watercolor painting by Anton Schönborn. From Hayden, *Twelfth Annual Geological Report.*

wounded a Dragoon Horse. The [load?] was slugs and it cannot be told how serious it may prove, but we may consider it providential that a man was not injured. The horse got into camp and may be able to go on.

Three or four antelope were killed today, giving us a full supply of fresh meat for present wants, and on the opposite hills four buffalo were seen as we came to the river, giving us hopes that we will soon have game in abundance.

I now have every reason to hope that we will reach the 3 forks this week, and if Lt. M[aynadier] does so, I shall start for the Eclipse on Monday next.

Tuesday, June 26

While at breakfast this morning the Doctor was hastily called to see one of the men who had shot himself. It proved to be Theodore [Montoy?], one of our packers who it seems was wiping a loaded gun. The iron ram rod had struck him just below the right nipple and passing through the fleshy part of the breast and come out a little in front of the point of the right shoulder, glancing on the shoulder bone. At first it was thought to have penetrated the vitals, but it was soon found to be only a flesh wound and the Dr. [*Hayden*] pronounced it not serious. Providentially, the ram rod broke and the wiper and ball remained wedged in the gun about six inches from the muzzle.

The herd was being driven up at the time preparatory to starting. I immediately ordered it back to see the result. As soon as the Dr. pronounced the wound not to be fatal, I directed a litter to be prepared to carry him on, but a travois being recommended I determined to try it.[88]

By 10 o'clock all was ready and once more bringing up our animals we got started at Eleven.

Our course was down the Madison. The valley is from one to two miles wide and is composed of three very distinctly defined terraces nearly level—their sides being very steep. Frequently these terraces run into each other, making it necessary to ascend or descend a steep pitch. In other respects the traveling was good. After traveling about two hours the Dr. sent me word that the wounded man was worse and requested a halt, which I immediately ordered having traveled only some five or six miles. I have had a horse litter prepared to carry him on and I hope he will now get along better.

Wednesday, June 27

Our camp of last night was in the forks between the Madison and "Ross's fork," and we had to retrace our steps this morning for about 1/4 of a mile to get onto the Indian trail for a crossing. A steep pitch brought us down to Ross's fork, after crossing which we continued our course down the Madison, the road being very much of the same kind as yesterday, now on one plateau and now on another passing up and down steep grades to get from one to the other.

About ten miles from camp the Plateau disappears entirely from the west side of the river and the trail passes along the steep side of a hill some 300 ft. high. Then passing down across a small bottom it again passes under a much higher bluff, the cragged rocks frowning down on us from above and the river rushing in a torrent at our feet. As soon as it was possible for the trail to reach the summit it did so and we found our selves on a broad level plain.

Stretching off to the foot of the mountain the road descended again several times to the river and rose again to the heights when compelled to do so by the rivers cutting into the banks. With these exceptions the traveling was good and the train made good progress. The musquitoes were so thick that there was little need of whip or spur. The face of the country is rapidly assuming the aspect of that on the Missouri near Fort Pierre and below, the rugged mountains are receding and the hills becoming more rounded and barren. The valley affords little or no wood and the grass is becoming more brown and scarce. Numerous small streams flow into the river, the banks of which are all lined by a narrow fringe of aspens, alders and willows, and these give the valley an appearance not unlike that of a large farm divided by hedges. {It is needless to add that the prospect is far less inviting.}

We had to travel some distance after I wanted to stop before we could find a camping ground, as the valley does not at all points furnish fuel enough to boil a cup of coffee. Where we now are a few drifted cotton woods and some willows furnish a scanty supply.

Our wounded man has got along finely, the horse litter doing very well after replacing one of the poles which was too weak and broke. He came into camp after the train (about half an hour) with the rear guard. Have made a march of some 25 miles.

Our hunter got three antelope today which keeps up our supply of fresh meat. But our other supplies are fast giving out.

We passed one or two small snow banks today which shows that the drifts of the past winter must have been very deep.

Thursday, June 28

Continued our course down the Madison. For the first six miles we kept in the river bottom and had numerous sloughs and muddy little streams to pass. A narrow fringe of cotton woods and willows borders most parts of the stream. While in the bottom, two buffalo were seen on the opposite bank. When they caught sight of us they rushed off down the stream and, crossing it in advance of the train, rose the hill just in time to come in contact with our hunter, who killed one of them, giving the first buffalo meat we have had this season. After leaving the river bottom we traveled on the 1st plateau and found more firm footing, our course diverging slightly from the river which bears off to the right towards a cañon through a range of broken hills that stretches across the valley making "a hole" of the upper part of the valley of the Madison very similar but larger than Pierre's or Jackson's holes.

Heretofore [*illegible word*] the valley has been widening out all the way down, and at our last night's camp the mountains are some 15 miles apart. The tops are rugged and in many places covered with snow. They then slope down rapidly to the 1st plateau—then drop down by irregular steps to the river bank. All the plateaus are covered with a luxuriant growth of bunch grass, and at this season would afford grazing grounds for large numbers of cattle. Antelope in large numbers are now almost the sole occupants.

After reaching the 1st plateau we continued our course to the foot of the range of hills that cross the valley and encamped about 4 miles from the mouth of a small stream that flows in to the Madison from the mountains to our left. The bottom of this stream is a mile wide and wet and marshy—but as our camp is on the foot slopes of the hills we are on dry ground. Would have traveled further but was fearful of going over the hills after having moved 18 miles.

Friday, June 29

Commenced this morning to go over the hills that have intercepted our views for the last two days. A long gradual slope of about 5 miles brought us to the top of the 1st range. Then descending across the valley and down a small stream flowing to the left across our path commenced a second rise, and after having traveled some 10 or 12 miles reached a point from which we got our first view of the 3 forks of the Missouri.

After passing some five miles further over the hills we looked down on the level plain where the Jefferson, Madison and Gallatin rivers meet. It was distant, but no camping ground was at hand and I determined to push on. We reached the Madison at 5 PM having traveled 10 hours and made {a very unusual distance during the day of} about 35 miles. The valley at this point is wide and much of it wet. The Madison flows in a winding channel much cut up by islands and sloughs. The barometer indicates a fall of near 1000 ft. since we left our last night's camp. So that the Madison must be a continuous rapid through the cañon or have high hills upon it. And Bridger knows nothing of any perpendicular fall, but I regret now not having sent parties to examine the cañon through its whole length if that had been possible.

Considerable timber is growing on the Jefferson and some little on the Madison, but most of it is on the sides next to the bluff; indeed, where we are now it is difficult to get wood enough for cooking purposes.

We see no signs of Lt. Maynadier's party and I fear they will not be here in time for me to go to the eclipse, tho I cannot feel that any serious accident could have happened to them.

Rain and thick clouds prevented my observing tonight.

Saturday, June 30

Sent a small party to look for a crossing of the Jefferson fork and all the rest of the men to getting out timber for a boat. For even should we be able to ford, the boat will be wanted to communicate with Lt. M, when he arrives. I went with Dr. Hayden to look for a better camping ground and possibly to find a place to cross. We passed over to the Jefferson and down to where it and the Madison unite. Found good ground for camping at a point about 400 yards above the junction of the two rivers and on a narrow neck only 37 paces across.

On getting back to camp we found the [*illegible word*] for the boat all out and the party sent up the river. Reported a point found where the Jefferson could be forded by animals but too deep for packs. So I concluded to move to the point I found and boat it from there sending the animals around to the ford already found.

A rain storm came up just as we were getting ready to move and delayed operations about an hour. After it was over we got to our new camp and commenced putting our boat together.

The valley of 3 forks have been well described by Lewis and Clark. I ascended a hill near our morning's camp {and read the details of their journal} looking at the scene.[89] Every part could be recognized, even the point mentioned by them as favorable for a fortification was in sight. But I doubt if it would be selected for such purposes even if one were to be built, as it is commanded by higher hills and could be easily taken. But it would defend perfectly the cañon that the Missouri enters immediately below, if that was what was required.

My observations for Latitude put us in 45° 55' much north of L[*ewis*] and C[*lark*] and nearly as low down on Warren's map.

Sunday, July 1

Service at 8 AM. Read tract on a more convenient season. May God grant his blessing.

One of the men swam the Jefferson today and reports that what we are on is not the whole of the river. Two other streams as large have to be crossed. This fact with the non arrival of Lt. M makes me inclined to cross the Madison and Gallatin {instead of the Jefferson} and to go to Fort Benton {by the east bank of the Missouri river}; and should they not arrive before we get across, {we can advance towards the Yellowstone until we meet them and thence to Fort Benton. By so doing Bridger says we must meet up with them. We will be saving their

coming to the 3 forks and pass through a country less known than
to go down on the west side.}

Observed Lunar Distances for Longitude this evening, but moon
was so low I fear they will not amount to much. Day warm
and musquitoes very troublesome.

Monday, July 2

Set all hands to finishing the boat having determined to cross
the Madison and Gallatin rivers, and if Lt. M. does not arrive before,
go as far as the Yellow Stone, to meet him. Should he arrive before we
leave this valley, we will then strike at once for Fort Benton. While the
boat was making, the same man who swam the Jefferson crossed the
Madison and Gallatin and came back reporting that the Gallatin could
probably be forded.

The boat was launched at 2 PM, it having required some time to
mend the lodge skin which was found very rotten, having been put up
wet. As soon as the boat was ready we commenced crossing goods. Our
boat was a little larger or supplies much reduced and the river much less
formidable than the Snake River, so that crossing it was not as much
of an undertaking. All were on the right bank by 7 1/2 PM, the animals
having come across finely following a horse that was led by the boat.

Tuesday, July 3

Before setting out this morning I had a further examination made
of the ford of the Gallatin, it having been pronounced practicable. We
packed up and got started about 9 1/2 o'clock. The Gallatin was crossed
where it was separated into two channels, the first of which was very
rapid and about 4 ft. deep, the second not over 3 ft. in depth. We came
out about half a mile above the mouth of the Gallatin and at once
ascended the bluff and continued our course up that stream traveling
nearly East. After traveling some two or three miles we met the hunter
of Lt. Maynadier's party, who reported the command as being on their
way down and only five or six miles in advance of us. We met them as
they were crossing the Gallatin and in time to prevent all getting across.
He returned to the north bank and both parties encamped on a small
plateau under a high bluff about 6 1/2 miles from the 3 forks.

Lt. M. reports having had much difficulty in crossing streams,
and that he had been obliged to abandon all his wagons and carts and
that his ambulance containing 3 Sid chronometers (box), a sextant,

two barometers, all his assistants notes, his meteorological notes and other small articles had been lost in crossing the Stinking [*fork*], a fork of the Big Horn.[90] It was drawn by 4 mules which were drowned and the driver narrowly escaped with his life. It reduces our [outfit] of instruments so low that it will be difficult to get the observations here, after that we [*disassemble?*] to fix our positions.

We attempted to make observations for longitude by lunar distance, but the moon was so low tho nearly on the meridian that they were not as satisfactory as desirable.

Wednesday, July 4

Day spent in camp together comparing notes and incidents of our trips. Some little {demonstrative ebullitions of} patriotism were displayed by burning an extra quantity of gun powder, but we have not the means to go further.

I took a careful account of my provisions, and after issuing a short allowance for 15 days to go to Fort Benton, gave all the ballance to Lt. M. who says he now has enough to take him to Fort Union. If our supplies are at Fort Benton we will be well enough off; if not, our only resource will be game from there till we get to Fort Union. {The contemplated trip to the remote north into the line of the total eclipse, (north of latitude 52°,) on the 18th instant, I am reluctantly compelled to abandon.

There now remain but 13 days in which I could travel, while the distance is 500 miles. It would thus require average journeys of 38 miles per diem, which, considering the nature of the unexplored wilderness through which we should be compelled to pass, is manifestly impossible. Had Lieutenant Maynadier succeeded in rejoining me by the last of June, I should have attempted to comply with the request of the department, but unforeseen obstacles have delayed him four days beyond the appointed time, and as I did not feel justified in leaving the party until assured of his safety, this plan must be from necessity relinquished.

On leaving Deer creek (winter quarters) I had simply procured a three-months supply of short rations: one pound of flour and six ounces of bacon, with coffee and sugar, per diem for each man. A considerable percentage of this had wasted by the sifting of the flour through the sacks and the frying of the bacon under the sun's rays during the marches. Game has therefore been indispensable to the subsistence of the expedition, and the question of supplies is thus attended with serious embarrassments.}

Lt. Mullins will accompany me from here to Fort Benton, as I hope to be able to have both a Land and River party from there, and to give him the command of the land party as far as the mouth of the Yellowstone.[91]

Beautiful aurora {borealis} just at twilight followed by dark clouds which prevented observing.

EPILOGUE

Seeing Jackson Hole and Missing the Upper Yellowstone

Before highlighting the Raynolds Expedition's specific accomplishments and impacts, we believe it is important to address its place in today's western history.

Briefly: The Raynolds Expedition has become best known for something that it did do, even though it had not planned to do it, and for something that it did not do, although it had planned to do it. What it *did* do was to pass through Jackson Hole, becoming the first government expedition to do so. What it *did not* do was to explore that part of the upper Yellowstone that is now part of today's Yellowstone National Park. As Raynolds' journal and *Report* make clear, both the achievements and the nonachievements of the expedition were influenced by what the party encountered in the northwest portion of the Wind River Range.

After trying for a week to find a way through the snow from the area of today's Togwotee Pass north to Yellowstone, Raynolds and his party gave up and went through Jackson Hole instead, arriving in the valley on June 11, 1860. Because of difficulties crossing the Snake River, the party could not leave the valley, cross Teton Pass, and reach Pierre's Hole until June 18—a delay of seven days.

Raynolds' descriptions of the party's movements in Jackson Hole are, however, of special interest, since it was the first official U.S. government expedition into the area that would later include Grand Teton National Park. In addition, at least four images of the Tetons were drawn by the two artists in the party—probably the first-known artistic images of the dramatic Teton Range.

Historians wonder why the Raynolds party did not enter the upper Yellowstone area by some other route after reaching Jackson Hole.[1] Two alternative routes have been suggested. After reaching the Snake River on June 11, the party might have been able to go north on that river until it reached the sources of the Yellowstone River.

73

Alternatively, upon coming to the Madison River on June 25, the party could have gone up the river (southeast) rather than down it (northwest), thereby reaching its origin at the junction of the Firehole and Gibbon rivers about fifty miles to the southeast. This would have placed them squarely within what is now Yellowstone National Park.

Raynolds, however, had other ideas. As early as June 7, even before entering Jackson Hole, he wrote in his journal, "I therefore reluctantly concluded to abandon this route [*the one originally planned*] and tomorrow start for a more western pass onto the Head of the Madison. I fear the passage of the 3 Tetons range, but this or going back by Wind river is the only thing left."[2] In his published *Report*, Raynolds made it clear that his objective was to "seek for a route to the Three Forks of the Missouri" by these means.[3]

Did he consider either of the other two alternatives? Neither his handwritten journal nor his published *Report* gives any suggestion that he did. This is surprising, since one would expect that he would have discussed these options with Bridger. It leaves us puzzled as to what happened.

Our hypothesis is that these alternatives were not considered seriously because they conflicted with the expedition's strict timetable. Raynolds was, after all, committed to meeting Maynadier at the Three Forks by June 30. The plan called for Maynadier to temporarily take command of most of the party there while Raynolds and a few others continued on to that part of British America located north of 52° latitude (more than one hundred miles north of the border), to observe the solar eclipse on July 18.

Given the fact that Raynolds was now behind schedule, neither of the alternative routes through Yellowstone would have made this possible. He had lost valuable time stranded in the snow-covered area at Togwotee Pass; and once in Jackson Hole, he might have feared he would once again encounter snow while ascending the Yellowstone Plateau. He also became even further behind in attempting to cross the Snake River.

Ironically, Maynadier's division was not at the Three Forks on June 30 after all, arriving three days later and too late for Raynolds to head north for the eclipse. If Raynolds had not been committed to meeting up with Maynadier's division at the Three Forks on June 30, he might well have taken the extra time to go through portions of the Yellowstone area and thereby have led the first government party to encounter the wonders of what is today's Yellowstone National Park.

The Raynolds Expedition's Accomplishments

The expedition concluded in Omaha on October 4, 1860, and there it disbanded. The next day Raynolds sent a short preliminary report to Captain Humphreys that summarized his party's findings. It was published before the end of the year (see appendix 2).

Raynolds could not have concluded his expedition at a less opportune time for receiving the attention that he and his party were due. One month and two days after the expedition concluded, Abraham Lincoln was elected president. The nation was embroiled in controversies that would explode six months later into the Civil War. Those who served in the Raynolds party were undoubtedly caught up in this turmoil. James Hutton and Lieutenant Mullins soon joined the Confederate ranks.[4] Raynolds served the Union army with distinction, as did Hayden, who worked as a medical doctor in the field.

Raynolds's full and final *Report*—what historians most often refer to when discussing the expedition—would not be published until 1868. This was three years after the end of the Civil War and a full eight years after the expedition. During this time the many accomplishments of the expedition were never known or quickly forgotten. They are, however, in the public record, and historians can now more fully assess their impact.[5]

Not surprisingly, with the use of two divisions, and even a third at one point, Raynolds successfully explored and described large portions of the still unknown areas his expedition was assigned to investigate. Traveling more than 2,500 miles by land and water, he and his men charted a region of almost 250,000 square miles. Careful topographical notes were taken over all the routes, most of which were measured by the party's odometer. Meteorological and barometrical observations were also made to give profiles of all lines of travel, along with nightly astronomical observations whenever the weather permitted.

Raynolds' *Report* identified mineralogical and agricultural resources, navigable streams, and the possible locations for future roads and railroads.

For the first time the geology of the country was carefully studied, and large collections of zoological and botanical specimens, fossil plants, and vertebrae were collected. Before these collections were sent to the Smithsonian Institution, well-known eastern scientists were to examine them and then publish descriptive catalogs and reports about them.[6]

Raynolds also summarized important information about Indian tribes, including their locations and disposition. In his *Report*, Raynolds wrote that the Sioux and the Crows were the principal tribes inhabiting the area that he and his party explored during their expedition. The Sioux, he wrote, are "by far the most numerous and powerful. . . . Those to the south or near the Platte seem disposed to be peaceable, while those in the north are fierce, ill-tempered, and warlike."[7]

He expressed his lack of surprise at the "horrible atrocities" committed by the Sioux as he was writing his *Report* in the late 1860s. Raynolds was undoubtedly referring to the bloody fighting that had occurred along the Bozeman Trail to Montana, where Indians killed about 260 whites in the last six months of 1866. During this time, U.S. Army officers relied heavily on both the Raynolds and Warren reports for information about Sioux country as they resumed their campaigns against the Sioux.[8]

Raynolds was convinced that there could be no permanent peace with Indians until the policies of government were radically changed, including restricting arms and ammunition to them and not offering them huge presents after Indian depredations occurred and new treaties were undertaken. "This," he said, "is simply offering a premium for future outrages."[9]

At the same time, he complained that the Crows were justly distressed in 1860 that their annuities were not delivered to them in their own country but instead were taken up the Platte, where, in order to receive them, they had to pass through the country of the Sioux, their most formidable enemy. This, according to Raynolds, was evidence of "gross stupidity and carelessness, or something worse," by those responsible.[10]

Although Raynolds' map left the Upper Yellowstone area looking pretty much the same as did Warren's 1858 map, additional information not seen or known during the expedition found its way into Raynolds' and Hayden's maps and into Raynolds' final *Report*. This included the addition of "Elephants Back Mountain," today's Mount Washburn, placed south of the Yellowstone's Lower Falls and northwest of Yellowstone Lake. Where today's Mammoth Hot Springs are located there appears a "Sulpher Mountain," and at today's Mount Holmes appears a "Mt. Gallatin." Raynolds' map also confirms the location of the trappers' "Burnt Hole," showing it to lie between Henry's Lake and Mount Holmes. These additions to the map were undoubtedly based on information from Jim Bridger.[11]

Also, at the time of the expedition, the area around today's Virginia City, Montana, was known only as a common summer hunting ground for several Indian tribes and was not considered important enough to be included on a map. By 1868, however, Virginia City had become a thriving mining town of some 10,000 people, and it appears on both Hayden's and Raynolds' later published maps.[12] Thus, in assessing the accomplishments of the Raynolds Expedition, it is important to distinguish between the party's actual findings during 1859–1860 and the new and additional information that was later incorporated in both the final *Report* and the expedition's related maps.

In summarizing the expedition's findings in his *Report*, Raynolds also wrote about the destruction of the buffalo. When the party first reached the valley of the Upper Yellowstone, he estimated that forty or fifty miles of the area were covered thickly with buffalo. The ongoing wholesale destruction of buffalo, he claimed, was because female buffaloes "are always singled out by the hunter." Hence, the males in a herd always exceed the females, "in the proportion of not less than ten to one." The reason females were singled out, according to Raynolds, was that only the skin of females is valuable for robes. The skin of male buffalo over three years old, however, was too "thick and heavy to be used for anything but lodge coverings, and the flesh is coarse and unpalatable, and never used as food." He also believed that the "immense number of wolves in the country" were responsible for killing buffalo calves. He believed there might be some slight improvement if trading buffalo robes were prohibited and a premium was placed upon wolf skins. As for the buffalo, he added, "I think it is more than probable that another generation will witness almost the entire extinction of this noble animal."[13]

The Raynolds Expedition had other important achievements that were not included in Raynolds' official *Report*. Photographs, drawings, and watercolors made by the expedition's two artists were supposed to be published in it as illustrations. None, however, appeared. Copies of the artistic images by Anton Schönborn and James Hutton in this book are, with three exceptions, taken from small collections of their work deposited at the Beinecke and Huntington libraries. The exceptions are three chromolithographs by Schönborn that appeared, with no attribution, in Hayden's two-volume *Twelfth Annual Report* (1883) of his geological surveys.[14] Hayden, of course, knew about these images as a member of the Raynolds party and as an admiring friend of Schönborn's. Perhaps this was a way for Hayden to publicly acknowledge the artistry and historic value of the work of his colleague, who committed suicide in 1871.

In this volume, for the first time, the Schönborn and Hutton images accompany and illustrate what the party saw on this part of its historic expedition. It's worth noting that there may be more images in private hands. Before the expedition was even half completed, Schönborn had made "hundreds of sketches."[15] The question is, What happened to them?

Long after the expedition, Raynolds corresponded with Hayden as he prepared his *Report* for publication. The subject of these images often appeared in their letters. For instance, on November 19, 1866, Raynolds wrote Hayden that he did not want to send Hayden any of the images, for he trusted neither the regular mail nor other modes of shipping. Furthermore, he confessed that he needed them to refresh his memory as he worked on the *Report*.[16] Then there was Mrs. Raynolds, who "has several of them in our parlors doing duty as mementos & she does not like to part with them."[17]

Raynolds also reported that for some time he had been "looking for Schönborn's original sketch book" and intended to send it to Hayden, "but I cannot put my hand on it & have thought that you might have it."[18] Sadly, no sketchbook is mentioned again, nor is it included in the two repositories that now hold the expedition's images.

Also not included in Raynolds' *Report* were the reports by well-known eastern scientists who had examined and described the many field specimens sent to them by the party during the expedition. Raynolds even included the names and authors of these designated reports in his published *Report*'s table of contents. The locations of all but one of these important reports remains a mystery today, and it is not known whether they still exist at all. Thankfully, J. S. Newberry's wide-ranging "Report on the Cretaceous and Tertiary Plants" appeared in Hayden's *Geological Report of the Expedition*.[19] It is likely that Joseph Leidy's findings are integrated into his voluminous later work, *Contributions to the Extinct Vertebrate Fauna of the Western Territories*, published in 1873.

Broadly speaking, like the earlier Warren expedition, the Raynolds Expedition was important for bringing scientists into the last major unexplored regions of the far West. In them, "mountain man, soldier, and scientist merged in the surveyors' frontier."[20] Hayden helped to complete a scientific picture of the West that especially affected the fast-maturing science of geology. In particular, he provided the first official recognition of the probable existence of extensive volcanic phenomena in the Upper Yellowstone.

Hayden, clearly the consummate scientist on the Expedition, wrote to Spencer Baird (1823–1887), prominent zoologist and then assistant

FIGURE 14. *Canyon of Rapid Creek, Featuring Ferdinand Hayden Investigating a Rock Specimen.* Watercolor by Anton Schönborn. Yale Collection of Western Americana, Beinecke Rare Book and Manuscript Library.

secretary of the Smithsonian Institution, that "I consider my geological results are far more important than all I have ever done before."[21] Thus, it was not surprising that it was Hayden who brought the most recognition to the work of the expedition. He did so by writing and publishing articles about his geological and scientific discoveries, beginning as early as 1861 with an article in the *American Journal of Science* entitled "A Sketch of the Geology of the Country about the Head-Waters of the Missouri and Yellowstone Rivers." Raynolds wrote an introductory letter for the article, saying that he believed the final results of the expedition would add largely to "all branches of the scientific knowledge of the country."[22] Raynolds' statement represented a major shift from what he once saw as the overriding purpose of the expedition. As an army officer, Raynolds had seemed far more interested in locating and characterizing Indians on the expedition and in determining areas for future roads and railroads.

By the time the party settled into winter camp, a frustrated Hayden wrote to his Smithsonian friend, Spencer Baird, that Raynolds couldn't "quite appreciate my large views about the importance of various branches of science."[23] This was reflected in Raynolds' journal entries when he expressed irritation at Hayden's frequent investigations away from the party and its assigned route. But by the time Raynolds wrote his introduction to Hayden's first article, he was most likely recognizing that the expedition's scientific discoveries were what it would become most known for. He also may have realized that Hayden already had become the most visible promoter of the expedition's scientific accomplishments.

Hayden's best-known piece of writing featuring his expedition discoveries came much later, in 1869, with the publication of his 159-page *Geological Report of the Yellowstone and Missouri Rivers*. It is the first geological guide to the areas he had explored with both Raynolds and Warren. Its comprehensive and detailed analysis led historian William H. Goetzmann to describe it as, "in many respects, . . . the most important work of the Topographical Engineer period."[24]

Also in 1869, Hayden wrote a short article for the *American Naturalist* entitled "A New Species of Hare from the Summit of the Wind River Mountains." Hayden named the species *Lepus bairdii*, after his friend, Spencer Baird. This rabbit was later determined to be a typical snowshoe rabbit, but its "discovery" had created a good bit of excitement among American naturalists.[25]

Clearly, the Raynolds Expedition accomplished a great deal, and despite its seeming lack of public recognition, its work had significant and belated impacts on the American West. It provided Ferdinand Hayden with a splendid chance to find new evidence on which to build his geological theories. But it also intensified his determination to one day see and experience the Yellowstone basin that the deep snow on Togwotee Pass had prevented him from entering.

It took Hayden another eleven years to fulfill this dream. By then, two private exploring parties—one in 1869 and one in 1870—had been to Yellowstone first. But in 1871, Hayden's expedition became the first scientific and government-funded party to enter and study the area. Wisely, he took several former members of the Raynolds party with him. James Stevenson became the expedition's manager, and Anton Schönborn became its topographer. Just as in the Raynolds Expedition, Hayden insisted that a landscape artist, Thomas Moran, and a photographer, William Henry Jackson, accompany the party and record what awaited them in what was soon to be called "America's Wonderland." Hayden's findings, the enticing photographs by Jackson, and the luminous watercolor field sketches by Moran enthralled the public and convinced Congress to preserve this Yellowstone land as the world's first national park.[26]

Ferdinand Hayden's reputation as the country's leading geologist and naturalist skyrocketed after his Yellowstone expedition. His name was given to the fertile Yellowstone area now known as Hayden Valley; and for a time what is today named the Grand Teton was called Mount Hayden. Alas, the latter never caught on with either visitors or people living in the area. After several years, Hayden asked that the mountain's name be returned to the Grand Teton.[27]

Most westerners have long forgotten Raynolds' name, but it can be found on a Tertiary species of gastropods (commonly known as snails and slugs) named by Hayden *"Vivipara raynoldsana."*[28] Probably the best-known topographical feature bearing his name is today's Raynolds Pass, the passageway that Raynolds and his party crossed at the Montana-Idaho border on June 25 and which he at the time named Low Pass.

But there is still one far lesser known feature named for Raynolds. Tucked behind and to the immediate north of the massive Mount Moran in the Teton Range is a conical peak with an altitude of 10,910 feet. Belatedly christened in 1938, it is Raynolds Peak.[29]

APPENDIX 1

Raynolds' Account of His Activities on May 31, 1860, as It Appears in His Published *Report*

Thursday, May 31

We started at 7 o'clock, elated at the prospect of making our next halt upon the Pacific slope of the mountain. Bridger said that our camping ground for the night would be upon the waters of the Columbia, and within five miles of Green River, which could be easily reached. I therefore filled my canteen from Wind river, with the design of carrying the water to the other side, then procuring some from Green river, and with that of the Columbia making tea from the mingled waters of the Gulf of Mexico, the Gulf of California, and the Pacific—a fancy that the sequel will show was not gratified.

Our route bore up the point of a spur that reached the valley of our camp, and in some localities the road was rather steep, but on the whole our progress was good, and we advanced nearly three miles and ascended about 1,000 feet in the first hour. Then following the ridge, we had a gradual ascent and a tolerably good road for three or four miles among stunted pines, reaching at last a large windfall, which it was necessary to pass directly through, a programme involving much labor and liberal use of the axe.

We then commenced another rapid ascent and soon found ourselves in the snow. By making our horses take the lead by turns we forced our way through, and finally stood upon the last ridge on the Atlantic side of the dividing crest. A narrow but deep valley separated us from the summit, the snow in it being too deep for an attempt even at crossing.

Turning to the left to avoid this ravine, and picking our way through the stunted pines, we soon found ourselves floundering in the snow. Bridger, for the first time, lost heart and declared that it would be impossible to go further. To return involved retracing our steps fully half way to the Popo-Agie, then turning north into the valley of the Big Horn, and perhaps following the route of Lieutenant Maynadier to the Three Forks of the Missouri—a course plainly inadmissible until every other hope had failed.

I therefore determined to reconnoiter myself, and if possible find some escape from our dilemma. Dismounting, I pushed ahead through the snow, which was melting rapidly, and rendered travel both difficult and perilous. At times the crust would sustain my weight, while at others it would break and let me sink, generally up to the middle, and sometimes in deep drifts up to my shoulders. In some instance I was able to extricate myself only by rolling and stamping and in many places I was compelled to crawl upon my face over the treacherous surface of the drifts. After great labor I found myself alone on the summit of the Rocky mountains with the train out of sight.

An investigation of the topography of the surrounding mountains convinced me that if the party could reach this point the main difficulties of the passage would have been surmounted, and I therefore started to return and pilot them through. Following my own tracks for nearly a mile I came upon them, and found that they had followed me slowly.

My attendant, who was leading my horse, stated that he should think they had advanced two or three miles since I left them, making the distance I had pushed forward alone some three or four miles. I found myself very much exhausted, and my clothes saturated with snow water, but I succeeded in guiding the party through and at last reaching the summit of the crest. The descent upon the south side was gradual, but very difficult, the snow being deep, while at the few points at which it was gone, the ground was a perfect quagmire, and it was not until we had advanced some six miles from the summit that we found a scanty supply of grass upon which we could encamp in the midst of pines and snow.

The day's march was by far the most laborious we have had since leaving Fort Pierre; and wet and exhausted as I was, all the romance of my continental tea-party had departed, and though the valley of the Green river was in plain sight I had not the energy to either visit or send to it.

Our last night's camp was at an elevation of 7,400 feet above the sea. The summit of this pass is very nearly 10,000 feet, and our camp tonight is 9,250 feet, so that the whole day has been spent in an atmosphere so rarified that any exertion has been most exhausting.

The weather has been a mixture of smiles and tears. Two or three flurries of snow passed over us attended with thunder, while at times the sun shone out brightly, renewing our life and vigor.

To the left of our route and some 10 miles from it rises a bold conical peak, 3,000 or 4,000 feet above us. That peak I regard as the topographical center of the continent, the waters from its sides flowing into the Gulf of Mexico, the Gulf of California, and the Pacific ocean. I named it Union peak, and the pass Union pass.

APPENDIX 2
Yellow Stone Expedition
Preliminary Report of the Topographical Engineers,
Captain W. F. Raynolds, October 5, 1860

[Addressed to Captain A. A. Humphreys, Topographical Engineers, in charge of Office of Explorations and Surveys.]

Omaha City, N[ebraska] T[erritory], October 5, 1860

Sir: I have to report my arrival at this place with my party, having completed the duty assigned me by the department by instructions of April 13, 1859.

As has already been reported, my party left St. Louis on the steamer Spread Eagle May 28, 1859; arrived at Fort Pierre June 18. At this point a delay of ten days was necessary, to hold councils with the Dacotah Indians, and complete preparations for land travel.

On the 28th of June we set out, passing north of west to the Sheyenne river, which was reached at the distance of about sixty miles. Crossing the Sheyenne we continued our westerly course along the north side of the Black Hills to the head of the Little Missouri, and thence to Powder river; thence down Powder river to within about forty or fifty miles of its junction with the Missouri river;[1] thence in a westerly course to the Yellow Stone river, which we reached near Fort Sarpy, (a trading post of Messrs. P. Chouteau, Jr., & Co.,) about thirty miles below the mouth of the Big Horn. At this point we were detained two weeks, waiting for the arrival of our supplies.

From Sarpy trading house, the command moved up the Yellow Stone to near the mouth of the Big Horn, when I detached Lieutenant Maynadier, with a part of the command, with directions to make an examination of the Chetish, or Wolf mountains, and across Tongue river to Powder river, and up that stream to its source.

My own division passed up the Big Horn to the Big Horn mountains, thence along the base of those mountains, across the heads of the "Little Big Horn," Tongue, and eastern branch of Powder river, to the main branch of the last named stream; then up it and across the eastern edge of the basin of Wind river to the Platte road, at the "Red Buttes," which point was reached October 11.

Lieutenant Maynadier joined me the following day, having followed in our track from Powder River. From the "Red Buttes," the company moved eastward some forty miles to Deer Creek, where I located my winter quarters. After selecting winter quarters, a small party was sent under Mr. J. H. Snowden to make an examination of the country between the routes pursued by myself and that followed by Lieutenant Warren, in 1857, in going to the Black Hills. This duty was successfully accomplished, and the heads of both branches of the Sheyenne determined. In the meantime Lieutenant Maynadier was occupied with a part of the party in preparing winter quarters, while I visited Fort Laramie to procure supplies for the winter.

The party was not reunited until the 3d of November, and it was not until the 17th of November that we were able to occupy our quarters, previous to which the thermometer had fallen to 17° below zero.

The time in winter quarters was occupied in making observations with transit for longitude, and in computations and projections of the previous summer's work. As soon as the season was sufficiently advanced, a party was sent under Mr. J. D. Hutton to make an examination of the country from winter quarters direct to Powder river, for the purpose of determining the practicability of a road from the Platte, by way of the Big Horn mountains, to Fort Benton.

The notes of the previous season were duplicated, one copy being forwarded to Washington and the other deposited in the magazine at Fort Laramie for safe-keeping.

The operations of the past summer commenced May 10. Two, and a portion of the time three, divisions of the party have been at work during the entire season. Lieutenant Maynadier was instructed to proceed by way of the Salt Lake road and the Popo Agie, and join me at Wind river; thence down the Big Horn river, and to connect with my work in the Big Horn mountains, crossing the Yellow Stone, and to join me at the Three Forks of the Missouri; thence to the Yellow Stone, and down that stream to its junction with the Missouri.

My own division left the road at the "Red Buttes," passing north of the Rattlesnake hills and Sweetwater mountains, and south of the upper chain of the Big Horn mountains to Wind river, at the mouth of the Popo Agie, where a reunion of the two parties was effected.

I then passed up Wind river to its source. Finding it impossible to cross the head of the Yellow Stone, I crossed the main chain of the Rocky Mountains through the snow, and at the altitude of over ten thousand feet, to the head of the eastern fork of Snake river, and near the source of Green river, a branch of the Colorado. Passing down the waters of the Snake river, I attempted to recross the mountains to reach the head of the Yellow Stone. To do this it was necessary to keep close to the main crest, and to cross a difficult spur of the mountains between the forks of Snake river. The small mountain streams were all swollen by melting snows, which yet covered the whole range. After battling the snow and mud for a week, and leaving the party for two days, the summit of the spur was reached on foot. A single glance was sufficient to satisfy me that if I proceeded the loss of my party would be the result.

As far as the eye could reach nothing but snow and pines was visible, and as my guide (Mr. James Bridger, the oldest and most experienced on the continent,) told me that even if the snow was gone we could not get out of the pines for weeks, I was reluctantly compelled to change my route.

I then continued down the stream I was on, through "Jackson's Hole," to Snake river. This stream I found swollen and entirely impassable without boating. While attempting to find a ford, I regret to report that one of the men of my escort, Private Bradley, company F, second dragoons, was drowned.

We had no material with which to build a suitable boat, but by using an India-rubber blanket, and a piece of lodge skin, succeeded in getting one twelve feet long and three feet beam; by the aid of this all our outfit was gotten across after a detention of five days.

Leaving Snake river we crossed the Teton range of mountains through the snow, and descended to "Pierre's Hole," and thence to Henry's fork of the Columbia; thence up that stream to its source in Henry's lake. From Henry's lake we recrossed the Rocky Mountain range to Madison river, (the middle one of the three forks of the Missouri,) through a pass which I have called the "Low Pass." The approaches to it are so gradual as to be scarcely perceptible, the altitude of the summit being at least 1,500 feet below that of the South Pass.

Passing down Madison river, I reached the "three forks" of the Missouri, June 29, and was joined by Lieutenant Maynadier, July 2. I found that he had had difficulties to contend with as well as myself, having had to boat several streams, and having lost, in one of the branches of the Big Horn, an ambulance containing most of his instruments, and some of his notes, but was so fortunate as to have saved enough to give a map of his route.

It is a source of deep regret to me that the detentions we had met with up to this point, rendered it entirely impracticable for me to go or send in to the British Possessions to make observations on the total eclipse of July 18. The distance was over 400 miles, and it could not have been accomplished with our animals, in the condition they then were.

Having spent the 4th of July together, we separated again on the 5th, feeling that we were turning our faces homeward. Lieutenant Maynadier going by way of the Gallatin river to the Yellow Stone, and thence to the Missouri. My own party passing the east side of the Missouri, through the Belt mountains, and by the Great Falls, to Fort Benton.

At Fort Benton I again divided my party, and giving Lieutenant John Mullins, second dragoons, who commanded the escort, the command of one portion, directed him to make an examination of the country between the Yellow Stone and Missouri, keeping as near the dividing ridge between them as possible. With my own division I descended the Missouri in a Mackinac boat to Fort Union, near the mouth of the Yellow Stone, taking the requisite notes and observations for the purpose of projecting it.

The party was again united at Fort Union, August 12. At this point I gave Lieutenant Maynadier charge of the small river survey, directing him to continue his sketches to the mouth of the Niobrara, where he would unite with the land office surveys.

Resuming my journey by land, I was desirous of going directly from the mouth of the Yellow Stone to Fort Pierre, but owing to recent depredations of Sioux Indians, I found it impossible to procure a guide, and I did not think it safe to venture into the country without one. I therefore passed on the north side of the river to

Fort Berthold; here again I tried to get a guide, but fear of the Indians was so great that no offer I could make could tempt either white man or Indian to accompany us.

Crossing the Missouri at Fort Berthold, and coming in site of the river at Fort Clarke, we passed thence directly south to the Sheyenne, and thence to Fort Pierre without trouble or difficulty of any kind, and without having seen an Indian.

Still keeping on the west side of the river, the next point that we saw was Fort Randall, and from that point we passed by way of the mouth of the Niobrara and the valley of the Elk Horn, to this place.

From the foregoing sketch of the routes passed over, it will be seen, that though I have not been able to accomplish all that was desired, yet that enough has been done to give a general knowledge of the whole of the extensive field that was assigned to me, to be explored. Since leaving Fort Pierre, the different divisions of the party have traveled by land in the aggregate, nearly five thousand miles, almost all of which has been over routes heretofore entirely unknown. In addition to this, nearly three thousand miles have been traveled in boats.

Careful topographical notes have been taken over all the routes, and the whole distance, with the exception of from Snake river, by way of Fort Benton to Fort Union, measured by the odometer.

Hourly meteorological observations have been made during the day time, when the party was not moving. Barometrical observations have been made to give profiles of all the lines of travel. Frequent almost nightly astronomical observations have been made by both Lieutenant Maynadier's party and myself. The geology of the country has been carefully studied, and large collections in the natural history and botanical departments obtained.

To develop the full results of the expedition will require time and labor. As soon as I shall have disbanded my party, and disposed of the public property belonging to it, I shall, in compliance with my instructions, repair to Washington for the purpose of bringing up my work, and will report to you in person.

Very Respectfully,
W. F. Raynolds
Captain Topographical Engineers

NOTES

Introduction

1. Rick Reese, *Greater Yellowstone: The National Park and Adjacent Wildlands*, Montana Geographic Series 6 (Helena: Montana Magazine, 1991) 20.

2. William Franklin Raynolds (1820–1894) was born in Canton, Ohio, and was appointed a cadet to West Point in 1839, graduating in 1843. He served in the U.S. Army Corps of Topographical Engineers for nearly twenty years and later as an officer in the Corps of Engineers, in which he attained the grade of colonel. For sixteen years he was engaged in surveys of the northeastern boundary of the United States and of the northern and northwestern lakes, and from 1859 to 1860 he was in charge of the explorations of the Yellowstone and Missouri rivers. For his services in the Civil War the government bestowed on him the honorary brevets of lieutenant colonel, colonel, and brigadier general. George Cullum, *Biographical Register of the Officers and Graduates of the U.S. Military Academy, 1802–1890* (Boston and New York: Houghton Mifflin Company, 1891) 2: 155–56; J. J. Reynolds, "William Franklin Raynolds," in *Twenty-Sixth Annual Reunion of the Association of the Graduates of the United States Military Academy at West Point, New York, June 10th, 1895* (Saginaw, MI: Seemann & Peters ,1895) 43–45; *Official Register of the Officers and Cadets of the U. S. Military Academy*, 1843. Similar records can be found for Warren (June 1850) and Maynadier (June 1851) in subsequent additions of this Register.

3. W. F. Raynolds, *Report on the Exploration of the Yellowstone River* (Washington, DC: Government Printing Office, 1868), 4.

4. The Corps of Topographical Engineers was established by Congress as a separate engineering corps in 1838, when some thirty-six authorized officers were placed on an equal footing with the Corps of Engineers. Lasting until 1863, it was always a small and elite group with varied responsibilities, including topography, mapping, civil engineering, and leading surveys west of the Mississippi. See F. N. Schubert, ed., *The Nation Builders: A Sesquicentennial History of the Topographical Engineers, 1838–1863* (Fort Belvoir, VA: Office of History, U.S. Army Corps of Engineers, 1988).

5. Raynolds, *Report*, 3.

6. Raynolds wrote of this experience, saying, "On the 9th of May 1848 I was one of a party of seven who were the first to stand on the summit of the peak of Orizaba. It is hardly a part of my military history, but it was one of the events of my rather uneventful life." Raynolds, letter to "Dear Gen'l," June 8, 1867. *Biographical Register of the Officers and Graduates of the U.S. Military Academy at West Point, N.Y.* 3rd edition, vol. II, nos. 1001–2000.

7. Angus M. Thuermer Jr., "Mapping the West." *Jackson Hole Guide* (Jackson, WY), July 14, 1993, B7; John Daugherty, *A Place Called Jackson Hole: A Historic Resource Study of Grand Teton National Park* (Moose, WY: Grand Teton National Park, National Park Service, 1999), 63.

8. Raynolds, *Report*, 6.

9. Tom Chaffin, *Pathfinder: John Charles Frémont and the Course of American Empire* (New York: Hill and Wang, 2002), 95–135; see William H. Goetzmann, *Army Exploration in the American West, 1803–1863* (Lincoln: University of Nebraska Press 1959) for an excellent history of western surveys.

10. Gouverneur Kemble Warren (1830–1882) entered the United States Military Academy at West Point at age sixteen and graduated second in his class of forty-four cadets in 1850. He was then commissioned a brevet second lieutenant in the Corps of Topographical Engineers. His services in the West began when he collaborated with Captain A. A. Humphreys in compiling the maps and reports of the Pacific Railroad Surveys. Until 1859, he was active in mapping Dakota and Nebraska territories. Howard Lamar, ed., *New Encyclopedia of the American West* (New Haven, CT: Yale University Press, 1998), 1180.

11. Jim Bridger (1804–1881), a mountain man, fur trader, and guide, was born in Richmond, Virginia, and began his western travels when he was eighteen by accompanying William Ashley on his first expedition to the Rockies. Bridger continued his western explorations as a partner in the Rocky Mountain Fur Company from 1830 until its dissolution in 1834. Later he went to work for the American Fur Company, and for the next fourteen years came to know the vast western area from the Canadian boundary to the northern border of what is now New Mexico. Realizing the fur trade was declining, he went into partnership with Louis Vasquez and built Fort Bridger, which became an important way station on the Oregon Trail. By 1850 his work as a guide had greatly increased, and he continued to guide until the late 1860s. Bridger married three Indian women and had six children between them, all of whom were educated in missionary schools or convents. "So vast and accurate was his knowledge of western geography that Bernard DeVoto has called him 'an atlas of the West.'" Lamar, *New Encyclopedia*, 126.

12. Warren wrote Humphreys on November 24, 1858, about the importance of another expedition in his preliminary report of his Nebraska explorations for the years 1855, '56, and '57. F. N. Schubert, *Explorer on the Northern Plains: Lieutenant Gouverneur K. Warren's Preliminary Report of Explorations in Nebraska and Dakota in the Years 1855–'56–'57*, Engineer Historical Studies, no. 2 (Washington, DC: Government Printing Office, 1981), 10.

13. B. J. Earle, "What the Army Knew in 1859: The Context for the Raynolds Expedition" (paper presented at meeting, Belle Fourche, SD, 1998), 7.

14. This probably was due to the unexpected death of his father in nearby Cold Spring, New York, for it meant that Warren was able to spend more time with his family at a difficult time. It is not clear whether Warren requested this transfer or whether a superior officer in the army made an odd decision to reassign him after he had completed his map of the Trans-Mississippi West. However, Warren was clearly pleased by the reassignment, for in February 1859 he wrote:

> The death of my father has entirely changed my plans. I shall not now wish to go to Nebraska [Territory] again. I must stay awhile with my mother. His loss is a great one to us, besides my mother requiring me to be with her. I feel so sad about it, that all my ambition seems to have forsaken me. There was no person in the world whose death could make me so unhappy as my father's has.

Emerson Gifford Taylor, *Gouverneur Kemble Warren: The Life and Letters of an American Soldier, 1830–1882* (Boston and New York: Houghton Mifflin Company, 1932), 44.

15. Raynolds, *Report*, 4.

16. Ibid.

17. Ferdinand Vandeveer Hayden (1829–1887) was born in Westfield, Massachusetts, and when he was about twelve was sent to live with one of his father's sisters in rural Rochester, Ohio. He graduated from Oberlin College in 1850 and then pursued medical school studies in Cleveland and Albany, receiving his medical degree in 1854. During his studies his interests in natural history and geology grew through close friendships with geologists John Strong Newberry and James Hall and with the horticulturist Jared Kirkland. Hall arranged for Hayden to join Hall's assistant, paleontologist Fielding Bradford Meek, to go on a fossil-collecting trip to the White River Bad Lands in 1853, and their collaborations (along with those of zoologist Joseph Leidy) initiated dinosaur science in North America. After serving as a surgeon in the Civil War, Hayden continued his western explorations and also became an adjunct professor of geology and mineralogy

at the University of Pennsylvania. In 1867 he was named head of the U.S. Geological and Geographical Survey, during which time his surveys examined and mapped some 420,000 square miles across the western Great Plains and Rocky Mountains. More than forty living and fossil taxi have been named for Hayden. Besides Hayden Valley in Yellowstone, his name is attached to numerous land formations. Marlene Deahl Merrill, ed., *Yellowstone and the Great West: Journals, Letter, and Images from the 1871 Hayden Expedition* (Lincoln: University of Nebraska Press, 1999), 216–17.

18. James Dempsey Hutton (c. 1828–1868), an artist, photographer, and topographer, was born in Washington, DC, and was the younger brother of the notable topographical artist William Rich Hutton. His experiences as a member of the 1855 expedition of Lieutenant R. S. Williamson and Lieutenant Henry L. Abbott to find a railroad route from San Francisco to the Columbia River qualified him to assume the same duties for the Raynolds Expedition. Hutton joined the Confederate Army when the Civil War broke out and saw action at the Battle of Pilot Knob. After the war he moved to Mexico, where he died in 1868. Peter Blodgett, enclosure with letter to Marlene Deahl Merrill, December 11, 2008.

Anton Schönborn (1829–1871) was one of fourteen children, and his father was an "apotheker" in Saxony. Anton and several siblings emigrated to the United States, and Anton began to assist an older brother, August, an architectural draftsman in Washington, DC, who worked on a number of important Washington buildings, including the Capitol and the White House. In 1853 he joined the North Pacific Exploring Expedition, a coastal expedition to the Bering Sea, where he may have served as a meteorologist. He later worked with Hayden on the Warren expedition (1856) as well as on the Raynolds Expedition. After the Civil War he worked for the Corps of Topographical Engineers and surveyed western forts, painting quite detailed watercolors of them. He was the topographer of Hayden's 1871 Yellowstone expedition, but committed suicide in Omaha right after the expedition concluded, leaving it to others to work up his topographic notes into maps. Many of his watercolors of western forts are in the permanent collection of the Amon Carter Museum in Fort Worth, Texas. Merrill, *Yellowstone and the Great West*, 219–20.

19. Henry E. Maynadier (1830–1868) was born in Virginia, graduated from West Point in 1851, and was promoted in the army to brevet lieutenant in the First Infantry. At the time he joined the Raynolds Expedition he had assumed the rank of first lieutenant. Maynadier later fought with the Union Army in several Civil War battles, including Fredericksburg. In March 1865 he was promoted to brevet major general for "distinguished services on the frontier while operating against hostile Indians, and

accomplishing much toward bringing about a Peace with later hostile tribes." He died in Savannah, Georgia, in 1868, aged thirty-eight. Cullum, *Biographical Register*, 452. Maynadier's report of his division's work as part of the Raynolds Expedition appears in the *Report*, 130–54.

20. Raynolds, *Report*, 14.

21. Pierre Chouteau (1789–1865) was born in St. Louis and with a partner formed a merchandising and Native American trading firm. In 1831 he became a member of Bernard Pratte and Company, which was the western agent of the American Fur Company. With the withdrawal of John Jacob Astor from the American Fur Company in 1834, Pratte, Chouteau and Company bought all the Missouri River interests of the old firm. Reorganized in 1838 as Pierre Chouteau Jr. and Company, it conducted business from the Mississippi to the Rockies and from Texas to Minnesota until its dissolution in 1864. One of the most powerful men in the West, Chouteau also invested heavily in railroads, rolling mills, and mining. He became one of the leading financiers of his time and lived his later years in New York City.

22. After winning a brutal battle with Brulé Sioux Indians on September 3, 1855, at their encampment on Blue Water Creek at Ash Hollow in Nebraska Territory, General William S. Harney (1800–1889) then proceeded to Fort Laramie for a council with a delegation of Sioux chiefs. A peace treaty was agreed upon there in March 1856, after Harney threatened the Indians with continuing military action if any further depredations occurred along the trail. Jeffrey Ostler, *The Plains Sioux and U.S. Colonialism from Lewis and Clark to Wounded Knee* (Cambridge: Cambridge University Press, 2004), 41; Lamar, *New Encyclopedia*, 470.

23. Fort Sarpy was the last of the Crow trading posts of the American Fur Company. It was built in 1850 near Rosebud Creek and was named for John B. Sarpy, a partner in the company. Situated on the banks of the Yellowstone about twenty-five miles below the mouth of the Bighorn, it was abandoned in 1853. Roberta Carkeek Cheyney, *Names on the Face of Montana: The Story of Montana's Place Names* (Missoula, MT: Mountain Press Publishing Company, 1983), 103.

24. Raynolds, *Report*, 82.

25. Fort Benton, located in Chouteau County, Montana, was built about 1856 and first named Fort Lewis for Meriwether Lewis. It was originally a trading post, but the American Fur Company closed out its business there in 1870 and then leased the fort to the government. Cheyney, *Names on the Face of Montana*, 92–93.

26. Fort Union was built in 1828 on the banks of the Missouri near the mouth of the Yellowstone River, on the Montana–North Dakota border. Originally called Fort Floy, its name was soon changed to Fort Union. Its

location provided fairly easy water access to both Indians and trappers. Cheyney, *Names on the Face of Montana*, 104.

27. Raynolds, *Report*, 71.
28. Raynolds, "Journal," October 12, 1859.
29. Ibid., October 14, 1859.
30. Ibid., October 17, 1859.
31. Ibid., October 24, 1859.
32. Ibid., December 16, 1859.
33. Raynolds' account of his trial and his thinking about it can be found in "Journal," February 16–25, 1860.
34. Raynolds, *Report*, 71.
35. Leslie Shores, "A Look into the Life of Thomas Twiss, First Indian Agent at Fort Laramie," *Annals of Wyoming: The Wyoming History Journal* 77, no. 1 (2005): 2.
36. Raynolds, *Report*, 72.
37. We have included only selected portions of Raynolds' summary of winter quarters, and they appear here in a different order than they appear in *Report*, 73–78.
38. Raynolds' *Report* incorrectly refers to the Indian agent Major Twiss (1802–1871) as "Major Swiss." Thomas Twiss, the colorful and enigmatic Indian agent at Deer Creek Station, was born in Troy, New York, in 1802. He graduated from West Point in 1826, was second in his class, and taught there until his resignation in 1828. In 1828 he married Elizabeth Sherrill, who was in charge of a female academy in Georgia. The Twisses soon took over the school together and later ran several other schools for women. After a brief stint at business, in 1855 Thomas Twiss accepted the office of Indian agent of the Upper Platte District, then located at Fort Laramie, leaving his wife and three daughters in the East. He moved to Deer Creek and became an agent there in March 1859. Sympathetic to the Indians in his area and critical of government actions of pacification, he took up with an Ogalala young woman named Wanikiyewin, whom he called Mary. The couple had one daughter and five sons. Accused of not restricting the local trader Joseph Bissonnette from selling liquor to nearby Indians and also of giving Bissonnette goods meant for the Indians, Twiss resigned in 1861. In 1870 he moved with Mary and his family to Nebraska, where he died in 1871. It appears that his marriage to Elizabeth remained intact until her death. Shores, "A Look into the Life of Thomas Twiss," 2–12; Alban W. Hoppes, "Thomas S. Twiss, Indian Agent on the Upper Platte, 1855–1861," *Mississippi Valley Historical Review* 20, no. 3 (1933).
39. These unfinished houses had begun to be built by Mormons some years before as part of a way station on their trek to Salt Lake City. A few had later been finished and used by Major Twiss before the Raynolds party arrived.

Raynolds' Journal Narrative, May 7–July 4, 1860

1. A military escort from Fort Laramie joined the party, consisting of thirty men of the 2nd United States dragoons, under the command of First Lieutenant John Mullins. *Report*, 78.

2. Joseph Bissonette (1818–1894) was born in St. Louis. Of French Canadian descent, he came to the West at age eighteen and soon became a successful trader. He briefly served as a guide and interpreter on the Frémont Expedition, then returned to trading and also built and operated toll bridges on the North Platte in Wyoming. From 1856 to 1863 he set up and ran a trading post at Deer Creek, sometimes illegally dealing in liquor. Several years later he was appointed interpreter for the peace commission at Laramie following the so-called Red Cloud War. In 1871 he moved with the Brulé Sioux to northwest Nebraska, where he acted as a subagent and assistant farmer. In 1875 he traveled to Washington, DC, with Red Cloud and Spotted Tail. Susan Bordeaux Bettelyoun and Josephine Waggoner, *With My Own Eyes: A Lakota Woman Tells Her People's History*, ed. Emily Levine (Lincoln: University of Nebraska Press, 1998), 143–44n12.

3. This Upper Platte bridge was named Gunard's Bridge in 1859.

4. The Red Buttes are located just south of present-day Casper.

5. The Platte Road ran across present-day southern Nebraska and Wyoming and was part of the famous Oregon and Mormon trails, becoming a kind of primitive superhighway during the great wagon train migrations to the West from 1841 to 1866. Raynolds described the Platte Road in his *Report* entry for October 11 by saying it was "as marked as any turnpike at the East. It is hard, dry, and dusty, and gave evidence of the immense amount of travel that passes over it. We had not followed it a mile before we came upon an ambulance with ladies in it, bound for the 'States,' and we were very seldom out of sight of some vehicle upon this great highway." Raynolds, *Report*, 70.

6. A. F. Dickson, *Plantation Sermons; or, Plain and Familiar Discourses for the Instruction of the Unlearned*, (Philadelphia, PA: Presbyterian Board of Publication, 1856), 138–48. The Plantation Sermons were sermons intended for slave owners to read to their slaves. This volume was one of several volumes of sermons that Raynolds received from a Mr. Kneass on December 16, 1859, while the party was at Deer Creek.

7. Independence Rock is a huge granite monolith covering more than twenty-five acres in Natrona County. Thousands of early western emigrants traveling on the Platte Road carved their names, some of which are still readable, on the rock.

8. Rattlesnake Hills, in today's Natrona County, comprise a mountain range that climbs to 7,795 feet above sea level.

9. "Grease wood" is defined by Raynolds in his *Report* as a "species of sage." He describes a "picket pin" as a "large piece of wood" shaped like a picket and driven into the ground to hold horses. Raynolds, *Report*, 80. "Buffalo chips" are the dried dung of buffalo used for fuel.

10. "Bitter cottonwood" is a common name given to a number of narrowleaf cottonwood trees (*Populus angustifolia*).

11. Daniel Baker, *A Series of Revival Sermons*, (Philadelphia, PA: William S. Martien, 1846), 158–88.

12. This eclipse was considered by astronomers of the day as the most important eclipse of the century. It would be seen only as a partial eclipse in most of the United States, except for small portions of the Oregon and Washington territories. *New York Times*, February 25, 1860.

13. The party was in the vicinity of today's Riverton, Wyoming.

14. "Lake fork" was probably today's Bull Lake Creek. A dam creates today's Bull Lake. A rod equals 5 ½ yards, or 16 ½ feet.

15. Raynolds apparently did not know the size of these lakes when writing this entry, nor was any figure for their size provided later in his *Report*.

16. The party was in the general vicinity of today's Lenore, Wyoming—two miles north of Crowheart Butte.

17. The sermon was from H. Grattan Guinness, *Sermons*, (New York: Robert Carter and Brothers, 1860), 128–55. H. Grattan Guinness (1835–1910) was British and one of the most prolific writers of published sermons in his day.

18. "Geo" is probably party member George Wallace. Raynolds and his family lived in Canton, Ohio, at the time he enrolled in the U.S. Military Academy.

19. The second stream that the party crossed is today's Dinwoody Creek. Once called Campbell's Fork, the name was changed to Dinwoody in 1911 by the U.S. Geological Survey. Mae Urbanek, *Wyoming Place Names*, (Missoula: Montana Press Publishing, 1988), 54.

20. This campsite was near Red Creek.

21. These red buttes can be seen today along U.S. Highway 26/287.

22. The "forks" were the main and East Fork of the Wind River. The party crossed again near Blue Holes Creek.

23. The stream is Torrey Creek.

24. Otter Creek is now named Jakey's Fork.

25. The party was in the vicinity of present-day Dubois.

26. The drift spur was Stoney Point, and one of the Upper Forks was Du Noir Creek. The Indian wintering place was north of Hat Butte near its confluence with the Wind River and Crooked Creek.

27. The bold, craggy rocks were probably those of today's Pinnacle Butte and Ramshorn Peak.

28. The basaltic ridge is probably the semicircle of volcanic cliffs from Pinnacle Buttes on the west to Ramshorn Peak on the east.

29. Hayden and Raynolds were probably drawn to the impressive Ramshorn Peak and were interested in investigating the character of its terrain and rocks.
30. This fork is Du Noir Creek.
31. The "marshy valley" is Du Noir Valley.
32. Hayden and Raynolds likely soon realized that, given the late hour, they could only hope to get to the little crag at the southwest base of Ramshorn Peak (it can be seen on Google Earth). Thomas Turiano, e-mail to Marlene Merrill, April 26, 2011.
33. This deep ravine is the East Fork of Six Mile Creek.
34. The weather was probably responsible for Schönborn locating the camp's location too far north on Raynolds' map.
35. Raynolds' journal account of this day differs substantially from what he wrote eight years later in his published *Report*. For this reason his published version appears in full as appendix 1.
36. Their road was on a ridge south and east of Crooked Creek.
37. They began by following a ridge between Snowshoe Creek and the South Fork of Warm Springs Creek.
38. The deep valley was along the South Fork of Warm Springs Creek.
39. They were moving southward along the ridge above the east side of Warm Springs Creek's South Fork.
40. The party camped at today's Fish Creek Park, after traveling along what is now Union Pass. James R. Wolf, "General Sheridan's Pass: 1807–1833," *Annals of Wyoming* 71, no. 4 (1999): 38n35.
41. It is important to note that in this entry Raynolds says nothing about the "Continental tea party" or about sighting and naming Union Peak or naming Union Pass. He does, however, describe these things in his *Report* entry for this day, which appears in full in appendix 1.
42. Bridger refers to the entire Gros Ventre drainage as the "Gros Ventre fork."
43. The party was on the South Fork of Fish Creek, a tributary of the Gros Ventre River, roughly opposite Little Devil's Basin Creek. Wolf, "General Sheridan's Pass: 1807–1833," 38n35.
44. There is no existing evidence as to what maps Raynolds took with him on the expedition.
45. They were crossing the South Fork of the Gros Ventre River.
46. The party camped at Buck Creek.
47. Hayden believed he had discovered a new species of hare, and he considered it to be both rare and remarkable because it appeared as though the male had teats for suckling its young. The remains of this hare were sent to the Smithsonian Institution, where they were catalogued as #4263 and exhibited in 1872. (Personal communication from Bill Resor.) Hayden was probably responsible for naming the species *Lepus bairdii*, for the

Smithsonian's assistant director, Spencer Baird. He later described the species in an article for the *American Naturalist*; see Ferdinand V. Hayden, "A New Species of Hare from the Summit of Wind River Mountains." *The American Naturalist* 3, no. 3 (May 1869). These "rare" rabbits turned out to be typical snowshoe hares that raise their young in a fairly normal manner. Today the species is known as *Lepus americanus bairdii*. Merrill, *Yellowstone and the Great West*, 271n32; Ferdinand V. Hayden, *Sixth Annual Report of the United States Geological Survey* (Washington, DC: Government Printing Office, 1873), 667–68.

48. The sermon was from Dickson, *Plantation Sermons*, 149–59. This is Raynolds' first mention of James Stevenson's presence in the party, although Hayden met up with him at Fort Randall on June 13, 1859, and Raynolds consented to let Stevenson become Hayden's assistant on the expedition; Hayden to Baird, 13 June 1859, Spencer Fullerton Baird Papers, Smithsonian Institution. Stevenson (1840–1888) had met Ferdinand Hayden when they served together on the 1856 Warren expedition. After the Civil War, Stevenson became Ferdinand Hayden's consummate USGS survey manager until 1879, when he worked in the Bureau of Ethnology, based at the Smithsonian.

49. The fork was the South Fork of Fish Creek.

50. The party camped at Purdy Basin. Wolf, "General Sheridan's Pass: 1807–1833," 38n35.

51. The fork is Fish Creek.

52. A fetlock is a projection on the lower part of the leg of a horse or related animal, above and behind the hoof.

53. The large creek was the North Fork of Fish Creek.

54. This tributary was Cottonwood Creek.

55. The party's campsite was located near the confluence of Beauty Park Creek and the North Fork. Wolf, "General Sheridan's Pass: 1807–1833," 38n35.

56. This is the last entry in Raynolds' second field journal, now part of Raynolds' collected papers at the Beinecke Library at Yale University. Following Raynolds' daily journal entries, several pages appear with a drawing, an address, and a list of clothes and their cost.

57. Bridger was probably looking for an unnamed pass on a ridge between Cottonwood Creek and the South Fork of Spread Creek. The pass—still unnamed today—was labeled "Pass No Pass" by Raynolds. Thuermer, "Mapping the West."

58. South Fork of Spread Creek.

59. The creek was Maverick Creek.

60. The creek was Cottonwood Creek.

61. This valley was Maverick Creek Valley.

62. "One of the branches" refers to Red Creek of the North Fork of Fish Creek.

63. The party camped near the confluence of Fish Creek and Trail Creek—a recognized Indian trail from the Green River. Wolf, "General Sheridan's Pass: 1807–1833," 39n35.
64. Both of the expedition artists, J. D. Hutton and Anton Schönborn, created images of this scene. Raynolds believed that his *Report* would include images by the two artists as illustrations, but in the end it did not.
65. The river was the Gros Ventre River.
66. From Guinness, *Sermons*, 333ff.
67. The party was probably adjacent to today's Lower Slide Lake, caused by the Gros Ventre Slide of 1925. It was traveling near today's Gros Ventre Road.
68. The "hole"—another name for an enclosed mountain valley—was named for an early trapper, Davey Jackson, who knew this valley well. Daugherty, *A Place Called Jackson Hole*, 55–56.
69. The "bold butte" is the West Gros Ventre Butte.
70. The sunflower the party admired was balsam root, a wildflower that grows prolifically in the valley in June.
71. By following the Snake River north, Raynolds came close to present-day Moose, Wyoming.
72. Gutta percha is a milky, rubbery substance that comes from tropical trees and is still used as an electrical insulator and waterproofing compound.
73. The boat was launched a bit south of today's Wilson Bridge, just east of the community of Wilson, Wyoming.
74. In his *Report*, Raynolds revised the rapidity of the current to ten miles per hour.
75. In 1869, Hayden published a *Geological Report of the Exploration of the Yellowstone and Missouri Rivers*, based primarily on findings during his time with the Raynolds Expedition. In his entry for June 18, 1860, he claimed that the central portions of the Teton Range "are composed entirely of erupted material." Hayden was wrong. The Tetons are a classic fault block mountain range created by the concurrent uplift and down drop of blocks in the earth's crust. They are the youngest mountain range in the Rocky Mountains. Daugherty, *A Place Called Jackson Hole*, 15.
76. The stream they crossed was probably today's Trail Creek. The pass the party traveled across ran more or less parallel to the present-day Teton Pass.
77. Many people have speculated that the trapper Joseph Meek carved his initials into this tree; however, there was at least one other trapper with the same initials who might have done this.
78. Pierre's Hole had been a strategic center for fur traders in the second and third decades of the nineteenth century. Especially during the Rendezvous of 1832, hundreds of mountain men, fur company trappers, and traders, along with Indians, met there to sell furs or trade for supplies.

79. The "stream" is today's Teton River.
80. Both Raynolds and later Hayden (in 1871) placed a "Mt. Madison" on their maps of this area. Some years later it was thought to be either Mount Sheridan or Mount Holmes. In 1997 Rod Drewien, from the Hornacher Wildlife Institute, followed portions of Raynolds' and Hayden's 1871 Yellowstone expedition routes in this area by plane, car, and foot over a period of five months. He concluded that this "high snow clad mountain" is either today's Sawtell Peak (elevation 9,866) or Mount Jefferson (10,196). Merrill, *Yellowstone and the Great West*, 250–51n28.

    It is unclear what Raynolds means by "Head of the Madison." Strictly speaking, the head of a river is its source, and the source of the Madison River is at the confluence of the Gibbon and Firehole rivers, about fifteen miles inside today's Yellowstone National Park. However, it's not clear how much Raynolds knew about where the Madison begins. He may simply have been referring to the point at which they would reach the Madison. The party arrived there on June 25.
81. Henry's Fork of the Snake River originates at the outlet of Henry's Lake—just below the Continental Divide, between Idaho and Montana. Both the fork and the shallow lake are well known for their excellent trout fishing.
82. The spring was probably today's Big Springs, which has long furnished year-round water for Henry's Fork.
83. They were camping at present-day Mack's Inn, Idaho.
84. The party passed into Nebraska Territory—an organized incorporated territory of the United States that existed from May 30, 1854, until March 1, 1867. Nebraska Territory was created by the Kansas-Nebraska Act of 1854. Upon its creation, the territory encompassed most of the northern Great Plains, much of the upper Missouri River basin, and the eastern portions of the northern Rocky Mountains. See http://en.wikipedia.org/wiki/Nebraska_Territory.
85. South Pass (elevation 7,550 feet) is a mountain pass on the Continental Divide in southwestern Wyoming, about thirty-five miles southwest of present-day Lander. It was part of the route of the Oregon Trail, California Trail, and Mormon Trail during the nineteenth century and is today a U.S. National Historic Landmark.
86. Although Raynolds named this pass Low Pass, it was later named Raynolds' Pass, in his honor. Idaho State Highway 87 and Montana State Highway 87 pass through it today.
87. The pass leading into the Burnt Hole is today's Targhee Pass. U.S. Highway 20 passes through it today. The name Burnt Hole was later attached to the geyser basins on the Firehole River in Yellowstone National Park. Osborne Russell, *Journal of a Trapper*, ed. Aubrey L. Haines (Lincoln: University of Nebraska Press 1965), 161.

88. A travois is a transport device, formerly used by the Plains Indians, consisting of two poles joined by a frame and drawn by an animal.

89. The first official edition of the Lewis and Clark journals was published in two volumes in 1814 with Nicholas Biddle serving as editor. Only 1,417 copies were available for purchase. The next known editions of the journals appeared in 1842, when a smaller format edition was published as part of the Harper Family Library. This was reprinted seventeen times through the 1860s and was probably the edition Raynolds relied upon. http://library.lclark.edu/specialcollections/shortL&Chistory.html.

90. "Sid chronometers" are sidereal time chronometers.

91. Fort Benton was originally an American Fur Company post and was established in 1845. Later relocated, it was rebuilt and located on the bank of the Missouri River at the present town of Fort Benton, opening in December, 1850. Robert W. Frazer, *Forts of the West: Military Forts and Presidios and Posts Commonly Called Forts West of the Mississippi River to 1898*, (Norman: University of Oklahoma Press, 1965), 79. The mouth of the Yellowstone River is near Fort Union, at the point where it joins the Missouri River—just east of the Montana–North Dakota state line.

Epilogue

1. See especially Mike Foster, *Strange Genius: The Life of Ferdinand Vandeveer Hayden*, (Niwot, CO: Roberts Rinehart, 1994), 83–90, and David Saylor, *Jackson Hole, Wyoming: In the Shadow of the Tetons* (Norman: University of Oklahoma Press 1971), 98.

2. Raynolds, "Journal," June 7, 1860.

3. Ibid.

4. Peter E. Palmquist and Thomas R. Kailbourn, *Pioneer Photographers of the Far West: A Biographical Dictionary, 1840–1865*, (Palo Alto, CA: Stanford University Press, 2000), 317. It is interesting to note from the above listing that Lieutenant Caleb Smith, the subject of the court martial, also joined the Confederate Army.

5. Unless otherwise noted, the accomplishments of the expedition are noted in *Report*, 6–18.

6. Specimens were sent to: J. S. Newberry (fossil plants), Joseph Leidy and Spencer Baird (fossil vertebrae), George Engleman (plants), Isaac Lea (unios), Chester Dewey (carices), and a Professor Sullivan of Columbus, Ohio. The expedition's various specimens were eventually turned over to the Smithsonian. Foster, *Strange Genius*, 86.

7. Raynolds, *Report*, 16.

8. Raynolds, *Report*, 16; Lamar, *New Encyclopedia*, 1053; Goetzmann, *Army Exploration*, 491.

9. Raynolds, *Report*, 16.
10. Ibid., 17.
11. See Aubrey L. Haines, *Yellowstone National Park: Its Exploration and Establishmen*, (Washington, DC: National Park Service, U.S. Department of the Interior, 1974), 26, and Lee H. Whittlesey, *Yellowstone Place Names*, 2nd ed. (Gardiner, MT: Wonderland Publishing Company, 2006), 97.
12. Lamar, *New Encyclopedia*, 1172.
13. Raynolds, *Report*, 11.
14. The three chromolithographs are all from Part I of Hayden's *Twelfth Annual Report*. *Henry's Lake and the Tetons from the Summit of Low Pass* is opposite page 173; *The Tetons: Looking Down Gros Ventree [sic] Fork*, opposite page 206; and *Washed Bluffs on Wind River*, opposite page 224.
15. Hayden to Baird, 13 October 1859, Spencer Fullerton Baird Papers.
16. Raynolds to Hayden, 19 November 1866, Hayden Survey Papers, National Archives.
17. Ibid. Other now-missing images are referred to in Raynolds' letters and portions of his winter camp journal that are not included in this book. For instance, he wrote in his journal on December 16, 1859, that he sent his wife that day a Schönborn drawing of winter camp "and a daguerreotype by Hutton of myself."
18. Ibid.
19. Ferdinand V. Hayden, *Geological Report of the Exploration of the Yellowstone and Missouri Rivers*, (Washington, DC: Government Printing Office, 1869), 146–73.
20. Daugherty, *A Place Called Jackson Hole*, 68.
21. Hayden to Baird, 13 October 1859, Spencer Fullerton Baird Papers.
22. Ferdinand V. Hayden, "Sketch of the Geology of the Country about the Head-Waters of the Missouri and Yellowstone Rivers," *American Journal of Science*, 2nd ser., XXXI, no. 92. (1861): 229–45.
23. Hayden to Baird, 13 October 1859, Spencer Fullerton Baird Papers.
24. Goetzmann, *Army Exploration*, 424–25.
25. Hayden, "A New Species of Hare."
26. See Merrill, *Yellowstone and the Great West*, 203–11.
27. Foster, *Strange Genius*, 234–35.
28. See *Bulletin of the United States National Museum*, pt. 1, 53 (1905): 695.
29. Leigh N. Ortenburger and Reynold Jackson, *A Climber's Guide to the Teton Range* (Seattle, WA: The Mountaineers, 1996), 374; U.S. Geological Survey, GNIS, "Raynolds Peak."

Appendix 2

1. Raynolds should have written, "thence down Powder river to within forty or fifty miles of its junction with the Yellow Stone river" instead of "its junction with the Missouri River."

A NOTE ON THE IMAGES AND MAP

We first learned about Anton Schönborn's three watercolor chromo-lithographs that appear in Hayden's *Twelfth Geological Report* from Bill Resor, a Jackson Hole rancher and historian of the Raynolds Expedition. But we sought more definite confirmation since none of these images were identified by Hayden. We checked their style with the known Schönborn watercolor images of western forts that were done after the Civil War and are held by the Amon Carter Museum in Fort Worth, Texas. These fort images clearly confirmed Schönborn as the artist of the Hayden chromolithographs.

Later communications with George Miles, curator of the Yale Collection of Western Americana at the Beinecke Rare Book and Manuscript Library, further confirmed Schönborn's identity as the artist of the chromolithographs. He alerted us to salt print photographs that are part of the William F. Raynolds Papers at the Beinecke. On our next visit there we inspected these monochromatic photographs and found that they were, indeed, photographs of the watercolor images on which the chromo-lithographic images in the Hayden report are based. Unfortunately, the location of Schönborn's original watercolors remains unknown; there is even a question of whether they still exist.

The Beinecke Library contains images by both Schönborn and Hutton; the Huntington Library in Southern California contains a number of Hutton's drawings, but no images by Schönborn. The work of both these artists are used as illustrations and cited throughout this book. Both libraries have a number of other images that were made during the earlier and later periods of the expedition but are not included here.

The Raynolds Expedition map was included in his *Report*, published in 1868. Hayden's geological map was included with his *Geological Report of the Exploration of the Yellowstone and Missouri Rivers*, published a year later. Hayden's highly colored map is the same as the Raynolds map, except that geological features were added to it by the use of differing colors, symbols, and lineations—all done in compliance with the geological map standards of his day.

BIBLIOGRAPHY

Manuscript Sources

William F. Raynolds Papers. "Journals of Yellowstone and Missouri Exploring Expedition, from Its Arrival at Fort Pierre to Its Return to Omaha." June 18, 1859–October 4, 1860. Yale Collection of Western Americana, Beinecke Rare Book and Manuscript Library, Yale University, New Haven, CT. 4 vols. Original bindings.

Hayden Survey Papers. Records of the Geological and Geographical Survey of the Territories, 1867–79. National Archives, Washington, DC. 1966. Record group 57, microfilm no. 623.

Spencer Fullerton Baird Papers, 1833–1889. Smithsonian Institution, Washington, DC. Record unit 7002.

Printed Sources

Alter, J. Cecil. 1979. *Jim Bridger.* Norman: University of Oklahoma Press.

Baker, Daniel. 1846. *A Series of Revival Sermons.* Philadelphia, PA: William S. Martien.

Baldwin, Kenneth H. 1976. *Enchanted Enclosure: The Army Engineers and Yellowstone National Park.* Washington, DC: Historical Division, U.S. Army Office of the Chiefs of Engineers.

Bettelyoun, Susan Bordeaux, and Josephine Waggoner, 1998. *With My Own Eyes: A Lakota Woman Tells Her People's History.* Edited by Emily Levine. Lincoln: University of Nebraska Press.

Boone, Lalia Phipps. 1988. *Idaho Place Names: A Geographical Dictionary.* Moscow: University of Idaho Press.

Bulletin of the United States National Museum (Washington, DC), pt. 1, 53 (1905).

Cassidy, James G. 2000. *Ferdinand V. Hayden: Entrepreneur of Science.* Lincoln: University of Nebraska Press.

Chaffin, Tom. 2002. *Pathfinder: John Charles Frémont and the Course of American Empire.* New York: Hill and Wang.

Cheyney, Roberta Carkeek. 1983. *Names on the Face of Montana: The Story of Montana's Place Names.* Missoula, MT: Mountain Press Publishing Company.

Chittenden, Hiram Martin. 1964. *The Yellowstone National Park.* Norman: University of Oklahoma Press.

Cullum, George W. 1891. *Biographical Register of the Officers and Graduates of the U.S. Military Academy, 1802–1890*. Vol. 2, nos. 1001–2000. Boston and New York: Houghton Mifflin Company.

Daugherty, John. 1999. *A Place Called Jackson Hole: A Historic Resource Study of Grand Teton National Park*. Moose, WY: Grand Teton National Park, National Park Service.

Dickson, A. F. 1856. *Plantation Sermons; or, Plain and Familiar Discourses for the Instruction of the Unlearned*. Philadelphia, PA: Presbyterian Board of Publication.

Earle, B. J. 1998. "What the Army Knew in 1859: The Context for the Raynolds Expedition." Paper presented at Island in the Plains Conference, Belle Fourche, SD.

Foster, Mike. 1994. *Strange Genius: The Life of Ferdinand Vandeveer Hayden*. Niwot, CO: Roberts Rinehart.

Frazer, Robert W. 1965. *Forts of the West: Military Forts and Presidios and Posts Commonly Called Forts West of the Mississippi River to 1898*. Norman: University of Oklahoma Press.

Goetzmann, William H. 1959. *Army Exploration in the American West, 1803–1863*. Lincoln: University of Nebraska Press.

———. 1966. *Exploration and Empire: The Explorer and the Scientist in the Winning of the American West*. New York: W. W. Norton.

Guinness, H. Grattan. 1860. *Sermons*. New York: Robert Carter and Brothers.

Haines, Aubrey L. 1974. *Yellowstone National Park: Its Exploration and Establishment*. Washington, DC: National Park Service, U.S. Department of the Interior.

Hayden, Ferdinand V. 1861. "Sketch of the Geology of the Country about the Head-Waters of the Missouri and Yellowstone Rivers." *American Journal of Science*, 2nd ser., XXXI, no. 92.

———. 1862. "Contribution to the Ethnography and Philology of the Indian Tribes of the Missouri Valley." *Transactions of the American Philosophical Society*. Vol. 12.

———. 1869a. *Geological Report of the Exploration of the Yellowstone and Missouri Rivers*. Washington, DC: Government Printing Office.

———. 1869b. "A New Species of Hare from the Summit of Wind River Mountains." *The American Naturalist* 3, no. 3 (May): 113–16.

———. 1873. *Sixth Annual Report of the United States Geological Survey*. Washington, DC: Government Printing Office.

———. 1883. *Twelfth Annual Report of the United States Geological and Geographical Survey of the Territories*. Washington, DC: Government Printing Office.

Hill, Burton S. 1967. "Thomas S. Twiss, Indian Agent." *Great Plains Journal* 6, no. 2: 85–96.

Hoppes, Alban W. 1933. "Thomas S. Twiss, Indian Agent on the Upper Platte, 1855–1861." *Mississippi Valley Historical Review* 20, no. 3: 353–64.

Lamar, Howard, ed. 1998. *New Encyclopedia of the American West.* New Haven, CT: Yale University Press.

Mattes, Merrill J. 1987. *The Great Platte River Road.* Lincoln: University of Nebraska Press.

McFarling, Lloyd, ed. 1955. *Exploring the Northern Plains, 1804–1876.* Caldwell, ID: Caxton Printers Limited.

Merrill, George P. 1924. *The First One Hundred Years of American Geology.* New Haven, CT: Yale University Press.

Merrill, Marlene Deahl, ed. 1999. *Yellowstone and the Great West: Journals, Letter, and Images from the 1871 Hayden Expedition.* Lincoln: University of Nebraska Press.

Moulton, Gary E., ed., and Thomas W. Dunlay, assistant ed. 1987. *The Definitive Journals of Lewis and Clark: From Fort Mandan to Three Forks.* Lincoln: University of Nebraska Press.

Official Register of the Officers and Cadets of the U.S. Military Academy, West 1850), Maynadier (June 1851). http://www.digital-library.usma.edu/libmedia/archives/ oroc/v1843.pdf.

Ortenburger, Leigh N., and Reynold Jackson. 1996. *A Climber's Guide to the Teton Range.* Seattle, WA: The Mountaineers.

Ostler, Jeffrey. 2004. *The Plains Sioux and U.S. Colonialism from Lewis and Clark to Wounded Knee.* Cambridge: Cambridge University Press.

Palmquist, Peter E., and Thomas R. Kailbourn. 2000. *Pioneer Photographers of the Far West: A Biographical Dictionary, 1840–1865.* Palo Alto, CA: Stanford University Press.

Paul, R. Eli. 2004. *Blue Water Creek and the First Sioux War, 1854–1856.* Norman: University of Oklahoma Press.

"Raynolds Peak." Geographic Names Information System (GNIS). http://geonames.usgs.gov/pls/gnispublic/f?p=154:2:3154737159768013::NO:RP::

Raynolds, W. F. 1860. "Yellow Stone Expedition: Preliminary Report of Capt. W. F. Raynolds, Topographical Engineers." *Report of the Secretary of War.* 36th Cong., 2d Sess., Senate Exec. Doc. 1. Vol. 2, Dec. 4, 1860, 152–55. In *Western Americana, Frontier History of the Trans-Mississippi West, 1550–1900,* microfilm no. 4433. New Haven, CT: Research Publications, Inc., 1975.

———. 1868. *Report on the Exploration of the Yellowstone River.* Washington, DC: Government Printing Office.

Reese, Rick. 1991. *Greater Yellowstone: The National Park and Adjacent Wildlands.* Montana Geographic Series 6. 2nd ed. Helena: Montana Magazine.

Reynolds, J. J. 1895. "William Franklin Raynolds." In *Twenty-Sixth Annual Reunion of the Association of the Graduates of the United States Military Academy at West Point, New York, June 10th, 1895,* 43–45. Saginaw, MI: Seemann & Peters.

Ronda, James P., ed. 1998. *Voyages of Discovery: Essays on the Lewis and Clark Expedition.* Helena: Montana Historical Society Press.

Russell, Osborne. 1965. *Journal of a Trapper*. Edited by Aubrey L. Haines. Lincoln: University of Nebraska Press.

Sandweiss, Martha A. 2002. *Print the Legend: Photography and the American West*. New Haven, CT: Yale University Press.

Saylor, David J. 1971. *Jackson Hole, Wyoming: In the Shadow of the Tetons*. Norman: University of Oklahoma Press.

Schubert, F. N., ed. 1981. *Explorer on the Northern Plains: Lieutenant Gouverneur K. Warren's Preliminary Report of Explorations in Nebraska and Dakota in the Years 1855–'56–'57.* Engineer Historical Studies, no. 2. Washington, DC: Government Printing Office.

———, ed. 1988. *The Nation Builders: A Sesquicentennial History of the Topographical Engineers, 1838–1863*. Fort Belvoir, VA: Office of History, U.S. Army Corps of Engineers.

Shores, Leslie. 2005. "A Look into the Life of Thomas Twiss, First Indian Agent at Fort Laramie." *Annals of Wyoming: The Wyoming History Journal* 77, no. 1: 2–12.

Taylor, Emerson Gifford. 1932. *Gouverneur Kemble Warren: The Life and Letters of an American Soldier, 1830–1882*. Boston and New York: Houghton Mifflin Company.

Thuermer, Angus M., Jr. 1993. "Mapping the West." *Jackson Hole Guide* (Jackson, WY), July 14, section B, 1, 6–7.

Turiano, Thomas. 2003. *Select Peaks of Greater Yellowstone: A Mountaineering History and Guide*. Jackson, WY: Indomitus Books.

Urbanek, Mae. 1988. *Wyoming Place Names*. Missoula: Montana Press Publishing.

Utley, Robert M., ed. 2003. *The Story of the American West*. New York: DK Publishing Company.

West, Elliott.1998. *Contested Plains: Indians, Goldseekers, and the Rush to Colorado*. Lawrence: University Press of Kansas.

Whittlesey, Lee H. 2006. *Yellowstone Place Names*. 2nd ed. Gardiner, MT: Wonderland Publishing Company.

Wolf, James R. 1999. "General Sheridan's Pass: 1807–1833." *Annals of Wyoming* 71, no. 4: 29–40.

Woods, Lawrence M. 1997. *Wyoming's Big Horn Basin to 1901: A Late Frontier*. Spokane, WA: Arthur H. Clark Company.

Short Course and Field Trip

"From Terra Incognita to Topographical Maps." Ralph Ehrenberg and Bill Resor. July 9–11, 1993. Snake River Institute, Wilson, WY.

INDEX

fishing, 32, 36
Fort Benton, 32, 68, 70, 71, 90, 105n91
Fort Berthold, 91
Fort Bridger, 94n11
Fort Clarke, 91
Fort Laramie, 19
Fort Pierre, 12, 90, 91
Fort Randall, 12, 91
Fort Sarpy, 10, 87, 97n23
Fort Union, 12, 70, 90, 97–98n26
fossils, 19, 75, 95–96n17, 105n6
Frémont, John C., 4
fuel, 26, 28, 66

Gallatin River, 40, 67, 68, 69
*Geological Report of the Exploration of
    the Yellowstone and Missouri Rivers*
    (Hayden), 78, 80, 103n75
geology, 34, 75, 91
Gibbon River, 74, 104n80
Glenrock, Wyo., 11, 15
Goetzmann, William H., 80
Grand Teton, 50
Grand Teton National Park, 73, 80
grease wood, 28, 100n9
Green River, 49, 83, 84, 89
Gros Ventre Indians, 43
Gros Ventre mountain range, 12
Gros Ventre River, 43, 44, 45, 46, 49, 52,
    101n42; crossing of, 50–51, 103n65
Guinness, H. Grattan, 36, 100n17
gutta percha blankets, 55, 103n72

Hall, James, 95n17
Harney treaty of 1857, 9, 97n22
Hayden, Ferdinand Vandeveer, 21, 27, 40,
    48, 68; biographical information, 7,
    95–96n17; as doctor, 64–65, 75; expedi-
    tion to Yellowstone by, 80–81, 96n18;
    as geologist, 79, 80, 81, 103n75, 104n80;
    missing images of, 78, 106n17; photo
    portrait of, 7; Raynolds and, 78, 79–80;
    at Sabbath services, 45, 57, 62; species
    and topographical features named
    after, 81, 96n17; taxidermic and fossil
    collection by, 45, 96n17, 101n47
—works: *Geological Report of the
    Exploration of the Yellowstone and
    Missouri Rivers*, 78, 80, 103n75; "A New
    Species of Hare from the Summit of
    the Wind River Mountains," 80; "A
    Sketch of the Geology of the Country

about the Head-Waters of the Missouri
    and Yellowstone Rivers," 79; *Twelfth
    Annual Report*, 77
Heileman, Wainwright, 21
Henry's Fork, 59, 60, 89, 104n81
Henry's Lake, 62–63, *64*
Hines, Dr. M. C., 21
horses and mules: death and injuries to,
    24, 48, 50–51, 63–64; difficult traveling
    by, 24, 28, 30, 46; disappearance of, 25;
    feeding of, 13, 24, 26, 27, 28, 44; fitting
    of, 20; Indians' stealing of, 26, 45;
    packing of, 23; purchase of, 19; in river
    crossings, 43, 50–51, 56
Humphreys, Andrew Atkinson, 4, 5, 9, 15,
    25, 75, 87
hunting, 25; antelope, 26, 28, 62, 64; bear,
    61; buffalo, 66; deer, 36, 45, 49, 52, 62;
    elk, 35, 36; as indispensable to expedi-
    tion, 70–71
Hutton, James Dempsey, 21, 32, 34, 35, 48,
    53, 54, 88; as artist, 8, 50, 77–78, 103n64;
    biographical information, 96n18; in
    Confederate Army, 75, 86n18; drawings
    by, *16, 18, 41, 50, 51*; photograph by, *9*

Independence Rock, 25, 99n7
Indians, 27, 28; Arapaho, 11, 15, 26;
    Blackfeet, 53; Cheyenne, 15; Crow, 76;
    Gros Ventre, 43; Harney treaty with, 9,
    97n22; horse stealing by, 26, 45; Hutton
    photo of, *9*; Raynolds opinions about,
    76, 90; Shoshones, 26; Sioux, 15, 76,
    90; Snake, 41, 53, 57; visits to Raynolds
    camp by, 53, 55, 57
Indian trails, 12, 49, 52, 58, 61, 103n63

Jackson, William Henry, 80
Jackson Hole, 3, 6, 12, 52, 89, 103n68;
    Raynolds' expedition as first to travel
    through, 11, 73; Raynolds party in,
    50–57
Jakey's Fork, 38, 100n24
Jefferson River, 58, 67, 68, 69

Kirkland, Jared, 95n17

Lee, J. M., 21
Leidy, Joseph, 78
Lenore, Wyo., 35, 100n16
Lewis and Clark Expedition, 3, 8, 68,
    105n89